U.S.-Latin America Relations:

A New Direction for a

New Reality

U.S.-Latin America Relations:
A New Direction for a New Reality

Report of an
Independent Task Force

Sponsored by the Council on Foreign Relations

The Council on Foreign Relations is an independent, nonpartisan membership organization, think tank, and publisher dedicated to being a resource for its members, government officials, business executives, journalists, educators and students, civic and religious leaders, and other interested citizens in order to help them better understand the world and the foreign policy choices facing the United States and other countries. Founded in 1921, the Council takes no institutional positions on matters of policy. The Council carries out its mission by maintaining a diverse membership; convening meetings; supporting a Studies Program that fosters independent research; publishing *Foreign Affairs*, the preeminent journal on international affairs and U.S. foreign policy; sponsoring Independent Task Forces; and providing up-to-date information and analysis about world events and American foreign policy on its website, CFR.org.

THE COUNCIL TAKES NO INSTITUTIONAL POSITION ON POLICY ISSUES AND HAS NO AFFILIATION WITH THE U.S. GOVERNMENT. ALL STATEMENTS OF FACT AND EXPRESSIONS OF OPINION CONTAINED IN ITS PUBLICA-TIONS ARE THE SOLE RESPONSIBILITY OF THE AUTHOR OR AUTHORS.

The Council sponsors an Independent Task Force when an issue of critical importance to U.S. foreign policy arises, and it seems that a group diverse in backgrounds and perspectives may nonetheless be able to reach a meaningful consensus on policy through private and nonpartisan deliberations. Task Force members are asked to join a consensus signifying that they endorse "the general policy thrust and judgments reached by the group, though not necessarily every finding and recommendation." Individual views and dissents that sharpen differences of analysis and prescription are also encouraged. Once formed, Task Forces are independent. Upon reaching a conclusion, a Task Force issues a report, which the Council publishes and posts on its website. Task Force chairs, directors, and members are solely responsible for the content of their reports.

For further information about the Council or this Task Force, please write to the Council on Foreign Relations, 58 East 68th Street, New York, NY 10065, or call the Director of Communications at 212-434-9400. Visit the Council's website at CFR.org.

This report is printed on paper that is certified by SmartWood to the standards of the Forest Stewardship Council, which promotes environmentally responsible, socially beneficial, and economically viable management of the world's forests.

Mixed Sources
Product group from well-managed forests and other controlled sources
www.fsc.org Cert no. SW-COC-1530
© 1996 Forest Stewardship Council
FSC

Task Force Chairs

[signature]

Charlene Barshefsky

[signature]

James T. Hill

Project Director

[signature]

Shannon K. O'Neil

Senior Adviser

[signature]

Julia E. Sweig

Task Force Members

Charlene Barshefsky

R. Rand Beers

Alberto R. Coll

Margaret E. Crahan

Jose W. Fernandez

Francis Fukuyama

Peter Hakim*

James A. Harmon

John G. Heimann

James T. Hill

Donna Hrinak

James V. Kimsey

Jim Kolbe

Kellie Meiman

Shannon K. O'Neil

María Otero

Arturo C. Porzecanski

David J. Rothkopf

Julia E. Sweig

*The individual has endorsed the report and submitted an additional view.

Contents

Foreword

Latin America has never mattered more for the United States. The region is the largest foreign supplier of oil to the United States and a strong partner in the development of alternative fuels. It is one of the United States' fastest-growing trading partners, as well as its biggest supplier of illegal drugs. Latin America is also the largest source of U.S. immigrants, both documented and not. All of this reinforces deep U.S. ties with the region—strategic, economic, and cultural—but also deep concerns.

The report makes clear that the era of the United States as the dominant influence in Latin America is over. Countries in the region have not only grown stronger but have expanded relations with others, including China and India. U.S. attention has also focused elsewhere in recent years, particularly on challenges in the Middle East. The result is a region shaping its future far more than it shaped its past.

At the same time Latin America has made substantial progress, it also faces ongoing challenges. Democracy has spread, economies have opened, and populations have grown more mobile. But many countries have struggled to reduce poverty and inequality and to provide for public security.

The Council on Foreign Relations established an Independent Task Force to take stock of these changes and assess their consequences for U.S. policy toward Latin America. The Task Force finds that the long-standing focus on trade, democracy, and drugs, while still relevant, is inadequate. The Task Force recommends reframing policy around four critical areas—poverty and inequality, public security, migration, and energy security—that are of immediate concern to Latin America's governments and citizens.

The Task Force urges that U.S. efforts to address these challenges be made in coordination with multilateral institutions, civil society organizations, governments, and local leaders. By focusing on areas of mutual concern, the United States and Latin American countries can develop a partnership that supports regional initiatives and the countries' own progress. Such a partnership would also promote U.S. objectives of fostering stability, prosperity, and democracy throughout the hemisphere.

On behalf of the Council on Foreign Relations, I wish to thank Task Force chairs Charlene Barshefsky and James T. Hill, two distinguished public servants with deep knowledge of the region. Their intellect and leadership ably guided the Task Force toward consensus. The Council is also indebted to the Task Force membership, a diverse group comprising many of our nation's preeminent scholars, business leaders, and policy practitioners focused on Latin America. Each member's input and insight contributed much to the report. Finally, I wish to thank Julia E. Sweig, the Nelson and David Rockefeller senior fellow and director of Latin America studies at the Council, for generously offering her support and guidance, and Shannon K. O'Neil, the Council's fellow for Latin America studies, for skillfully and professionally directing this project. The hard work of all those involved has produced an authoritative report that examines changes in Latin America and in U.S. influence there, while taking account of the region's enduring importance to the United States. I expect its agenda for renewed U.S. engagement to influence policy during the upcoming presidential transition and for years to come.

Richard N. Haass
President
Council on Foreign Relations
May 2008

Acknowledgments

Shortly after joining the Council as a fellow, it was my great pleasure to take on the direction of this Independent Task Force on U.S.-Latin America relations.

With the immodest goal of creating a new blueprint for hemispheric relations, the Task Force has benefited tremendously from the guidance of its two eminent chairs, Charlene Barshefsky and James T. Hill. Not only did they bring their own significant experience and expertise on the region to the table, but they also deftly guided the larger group in the exchange of ideas and in working toward achieving consensus on a broad range of issues. Julia E. Sweig, senior adviser and executive editor to the project, was instrumental in shaping this report, providing ideas, guidance, and support over the yearlong tenure of the Task Force.

In addition to our distinguished Task Force members and observers, this report benefited from the information and opinions generously shared by a wide range of individuals during trips to Bolivia and Brazil. Ambassador Gustavo Guzman, Ivan C. Rebolledo, and Eduardo A. Gamarra were particularly helpful during our trip to Bolivia, as was Paulo Sotero during our visit to Brazil. The Task Force also benefited greatly from conversations with and presentations by Jorge Castañeda, Wolf Grabendorff, Rebeca Grynspan, Peter Hakim, Celso Lafer, Luiz Felipe Lampreia, Doris M. Meissner, Maria Otero, Ambassador Antonio Patriota, Arturo C. Porzecanski, David J. Rothkopf, Ambassador Arturo Sarukhan, Admiral James G. Stavridis, and Roberto A. Suro.

The success of this effort relied on many Council staff. Sebastian Chaskel and Jacyln Berfond ably conducted extensive research to support the findings, and Michael Bustamante and Daniel Kurtz-Phelan each drafted segments of the report. Dan also deserves recognition for his masterful editing job, and Sebastian for helping guide the Task Force through many revisions and through its launch and distribution. Leigh Gusts and the library staff helped us find much of the information needed for the writing, and Council Fellows Laurie A. Garrett, Michael A. Levi, and David G. Victor all lent their expertise at important moments. Lee Feinstein and Lindsay Workman and then Anya Schmemann and Swetha Sridharan skillfully shepherded the Task Force from start to finish, providing a critical eye when necessary and coordinating closely with the Council's various departments. Once completed, Patricia Lee Dorff and Lia Norton took the written document and polished it into a Task Force report.

Along the way, Irina A. Faskianos led the Council's National Program in setting up meetings spanning six cities from Los Angeles to Boston, while Nancy D. Bodurtha and Kay King led the Meetings departments in organizing preview and release events for Council members in New York and Washington, DC. Lisa Shields and the Communications team and the Corporate and Outreach programs worked hard to get the report into the right hands, as did Kay and her able team in Washington, DC.

We are particularly grateful to Council President Richard N. Haass for convening this Task Force and to Director of Studies Gary Samore, who supported this initiative, which has allowed us to work closely with many Council staff and members and the broader policy community in the effort to substantially rethink U.S.-Latin America relations.

This project was made possible by David M. Rubenstein's support for the Task Force program. The Council also expresses its thanks to the Ford Foundation and the W.K. Kellogg Foundation for their support for the Latin America studies program. Now completed, our hope is that this report will lay the groundwork for new conversations, and new U.S. policies, transforming U.S.-Latin America relations for the better.

Shannon O'Neil
Project Director

South America

Source: CIA World Factbook, https://www.cia.gov/library/publications/the-world-factbook/reference_maps/south_america.html.

Mexico, Central America, and the Caribbean

Source: CIA World Factbook, https://www.cia.gov/library/publications/the-world-factbook/reference_maps/central_america.html.

List of Acronyms

DEA	Drug Enforcement Administration
DHS	Department of Homeland Security
DR-CAFTA	Dominican Republic and Central America Free Trade Agreement
FARC	Fuerzas Armadas Revolucionarias de Colombia
FinCEN	Financial Crimes Enforcement Network
FTAA	Free Trade Area of the Americas
G20	Group of 20
GDP	gross domestic product
IDB	Inter-American Development Bank
IEA	International Energy Agency
IMF	International Monetary Fund
IRCA	Immigration Reform and Control Act
LNG	liquefied natural gas
MCA	Millennium Challenge Account
NAEWG	North America Energy Working Group
NAFTA	North American Free Trade Agreement
NGO	nongovernmental organization
OAS	Organization of American States
OECD	Organization for Economic Cooperation and Development
PDVSA	Petróleos de Venezuela
PEMEX	Petróleos Mexicanos
USAID	U.S. Agency for International Development
VAT	value-added taxes
WHO	World Health Organization

Task Force Report

Executive Summary

This Task Force report takes stock of the current situation in Latin America and the main challenges and opportunities for U.S.-Latin America relations. Latin America has benefited greatly in recent years from democratic opening, stable economic policies, and increasing growth. Many countries are taking advantage of these developments to consolidate democratic institutions, broaden economic opportunities, and better serve their citizens. Yet Latin American nations face daunting challenges as they integrate into global markets and work to strengthen historically weak state institutions. These challenges increasingly matter for the United States, as deepening economic and social ties link U.S. well-being to the region's stability and development.

Rather than an exhaustive study of U.S.-Latin America relations and policies, this report does not reprise many long-standing initiatives or the intricacies of each bilateral relationship. Nor, given Latin America's complexity and level of development, does it seek to define the entire U.S. approach with one overarching grand idea. Instead, the Task Force identifies four critical issues and four strategic relationships that merit special attention at this point in time. Poverty and inequality, public security, human mobility, and energy security represent fundamental challenges and opportunities for the region and for U.S.-Latin America relations. These factors affect traditional U.S. objectives of democracy promotion, economic expansion, and counternarcotics. They also reflect new policy issues arising from the increasing societal and economic integration of the Western Hemisphere. In addition, the Task

3

Force calls for the deepening of the United States' relations with Mexico and Brazil, and the redefining of relations with Venezuela and Cuba.

In pursuing its objectives through the concrete policy recommendations laid out in this report, the United States must focus its efforts and resources on helping Latin America strengthen the public institutions necessary to address the challenges identified in this report. In doing so, Washington should work in partnership with Latin American nations through multilateral organizations such as the World Bank, Inter-American Development Bank (IDB), International Monetary Fund (IMF), International Finance Corporation, and Organization of American States (OAS). It should also continue to work closely with civil society organizations and domestic and international businesses to create more inclusive economic, social, and political opportunities for Latin American countries and their citizens, which will benefit U.S. policy goals.

Achieving the ambitious goals of strengthening institutions and improving the lives of Latin Americans will require long-term efforts on the part of many participants, most importantly Latin American governments and societies themselves. Nevertheless, there is a significant supporting role for the United States. Expanding its policy framework and concentrating on strategic regional partnerships will best promote U.S. interests, enhancing stability, security, and prosperity throughout the hemisphere.

Introduction

For over 150 years, the Monroe Doctrine provided the guiding principles for U.S. policy toward Latin America, asserting U.S. primacy in the foreign affairs of the region. Over the past two decades, those principles have become increasingly obsolete. Washington's basic policy framework, however, has not changed sufficiently to reflect the new reality. U.S. policy can no longer be based on the assumption that the United States is the most important outside actor in Latin America. If there was an era of U.S. hegemony in Latin America, it is over.

In most respects, this shift reflects positive developments within Latin America itself. The region has undergone a historic transformation politically, with military-authoritarian rule giving way to vibrant, if imperfect, democracy in almost every nation. Economically, Latin America is now one of the more open market regions in the world and a crucial global provider of energy, minerals, and food. None of this is to say that Latin America has entirely overcome its history of political tumult or done enough to alleviate poverty, improve competitiveness and human capital, or correct extreme inequality. But it does mean that U.S. policymakers must change the way they think about the region. Latin America is not Washington's to lose; nor is it Washington's to save. Latin America's fate is largely in Latin America's hands.

A failure to acknowledge how Latin Americans define their own challenges has created new political strains in recent years. It has also caused U.S. policymakers to overlook the ways in which the United

States can meaningfully contribute to Latin America's progress—furthering the United States' own interests in the process. By truly beginning to engage Latin America on its own terms, Washington can mark the start of a new era in U.S.-Latin America relations.

It is a cliché to bemoan Americans' lack of interest in Latin America. Still, this disinterest remains vexing given the region's proximity to the United States and the remarkable interconnectedness of U.S. and Latin American economies and societies. In recent years, as Washington's attention has been focused on crises elsewhere in the world, the connections have only deepened. From 1996 to 2006, total U.S. merchandise trade with Latin America grew by 139 percent, compared to 96 percent for Asia and 95 percent for the European Union (EU).[1] In 2006, the United States exported $223 billion worth of goods to Latin American consumers (compared with $55 billion to China).[2] Latin America is the United States' most important external source of oil, accounting for nearly 30 percent of imports (compared with 20 percent from the Middle East), as well as its main source of illegal narcotics. And as a result of both conditions in Latin America and demand for workers in the United States, migration from the region has accelerated. Latinos now account for 15 percent of the U.S. population, nearly 50 percent of recent U.S. population growth, and a growing portion of the electorate—allowing Latino voters increasingly to shape the U.S. political agenda. Cross-border community and family ties, as well as the Spanish-language media, mean that Latin America remains part of many Latinos' daily lives and concerns. For all of these reasons, Latin America's well-being directly affects the United States.

But even with such integration, the opening of Latin American economies and the globalization of Latin American societies means that U.S. policy is now but one of several competing factors capable of influencing the region. Latin American states, especially the larger ones, do not consider their interests to be primarily determined by diplomatic, trade, or security ties with the United States. Brazil has made inroads

---

[1] J. F. Hornbeck, "U.S.-Latin America Trade: Recent Trends," Congressional Research Service, May 18, 2007, available at http://www.nationalaglawcenter.org/assets/crs/98-840.pdf.

[2] "Trade in Goods (Imports, Exports and Trade Balance) with China," Foreign Trade Statistics, U.S. Census Bureau, available at http://www.census.gov/foreign-trade/balance/c5700.html#2006.

into groupings such as the South-South Dialogue with South Africa and India and the Group of 20 (G20), while countries such as Chile and Mexico have struck trade and investment agreements with the EU and a number of Asian countries, China most prominently.

The economic and political diversification of Latin America is reflected in Latin American attitudes as well. Esteem for U.S. global and hemispheric leadership is at its lowest level in the region in recent memory. In 2002, according to the Pew Global Attitudes Project, 82 percent of Venezuelans, 34 percent of Argentineans, and 51 percent of Bolivians had a favorable view of the United States; those numbers had fallen to 56, 16, and 43 percent by 2007. The percentage of Latin Americans who approved of U.S. ideas on democracy decreased from 45 percent in 2002 to 29 percent in 2007.[3] This general distrust of the United States has allowed Presidents Hugo Chávez of Venezuela, Evo Morales of Bolivia, Rafael Correa of Ecuador, and even Felipe Calderón of Mexico to bolster their domestic popular support by criticizing Washington. Most Latin Americans still prefer a mutually respectful and productive relationship with the United States, but the factors driving Latin America's desire for greater independence are likely to shape the region's posture toward the United States well into the future.

U.S. Policy—Past, Present, and Future

As the Cold War began to wind down in the late 1980s, Washington's focus in Latin America shifted from containing communism and combating left-wing insurgencies to three priorities: opening markets, strengthening democracy, and stemming the flow of illegal drugs. These priorities have remained remarkably consistent and largely enjoyed bipartisan support over the past two decades.

The focus on economic opening at first centered on agreements such as the Caribbean Basin Initiative (1983), the Andean Trade Preference Act (1991), and the North American Free Trade Agreement (NAFTA, 1993); negotiations for the Free Trade Area of the Americas

---

[3] "Rising Environmental Concern in 47-Nation Survey: Global Unease with Major World Powers," The Pew Global Attitudes Project, Pew Research Center, June 27, 2007, available at http://pewglobal.org/reports/pdf/256.pdf.

(FTAA), begun in 1994, are ongoing. U.S. efforts to strengthen democracy in Latin America began with President George H.W. Bush's role in the adoption of Resolution 1080 in the Organization of American States, which solidified multilateral support for democracy in the region. Both the rhetoric and substance of democracy promotion continued under President Bill Clinton, with U.S. policies designed to foster broad-based political participation and the development of civil society. In 1994, the Clinton administration sent 20,000 U.S. troops under the auspices of the United Nations to restore democratically elected Haitian president Jean-Bertrand Aristide to office. Over the course of the decade, it also actively participated in diplomatic efforts to avert direct threats to democracy in Guatemala (1993), Paraguay (1996), and Ecuador (2000).

The "war on drugs" escalated under President Ronald Reagan, culminating in the creation of the White House's Office of National Drug Control Policy in 1988, and continued to receive significant funding under Presidents Bush and Clinton. During the first Bush administration, U.S. troops invaded Panama to capture head of state Manuel Noriega for his involvement in drug trafficking; backed the Colombian state's hunt for Pablo Escobar and its fight against other drug cartels; and began a certification process to ensure foreign governments were cooperating with U.S. counternarcotics efforts. President Clinton inaugurated Plan Colombia with $1.3 billion in aid in 2000, with the goal of not only eliminating cocaine production but also bolstering the Colombian government's efforts to defeat a drug-fueled guerrilla insurgency.

When he was elected in 2000, President George W. Bush pledged to make Latin America a foreign policy priority. He announced several major new initiatives, most importantly a sweeping immigration reform that would be at the center of the U.S.-Mexico relationship. Yet since the terrorist attacks of September 11, 2001, American attention has been diverted elsewhere, prompting the charge—one also made against its predecessors—that the Bush administration has ignored Latin America's needs. The three pillars of U.S. policy toward the region remained, but U.S. initiatives have had mixed results. Congress ratified trade agreements with Chile (2004), the Dominican Republic and Central America (DR-CAFTA, 2007), and Peru (2007), but hopes for a hemisphere-wide free trade area have receded and agreements with Colombia and Panama have been caught up in U.S. domestic politics. Drug interdiction and eradication efforts have continued, with an additional $4 billion invested in Plan Colombia, but drug flows remain undiminished and drug violence in Mexico has escalated dramatically, prompting the proposal, in October 2007, of a $1.4 billion aid package to the Mexican government. U.S. involvement in the Inter-American Democratic Charter in 2001 helped further multilateral support for democracy, but a year later the United States was alone in the hemisphere in seemingly endorsing a military coup against Venezuela's democratically elected president, Hugo Chávez. This exacerbated tensions between the United States and Venezuela and—along with public statements by U.S. ambassadors in Bolivia and Nicaragua that were perceived as attempted interventions in the democratic process—undermined the credibility of U.S. democracy promotion efforts.

The limited success of many U.S. foreign policy initiatives threatens U.S. interests. Persistent poverty and weak state institutions have allowed the illegal narcotics industry to continue flourishing, while crime has escalated across much of the region. (Homicide rates have doubled since the 1980s, and rates of violent crime are now six times higher in Latin America than in the rest of the world.[4]) The seeming inability of liberal democratic governments in Latin America to deliver security, opportunity, and equitable prosperity has threatened to undermine public faith in representative democracy, encouraging the rise of politicians promising sweeping political and economic change. Much of the concern has centered on President Chávez of Venezuela. Since being elected in 1998, he has used oil profits to fund high-profile public projects and welfare programs while ruling by decree and systematically eradicating checks on his own power. More worrying in the regional context, he has also embarked on a campaign to alienate Latin America from the United States and promoted foreign policies that could destabilize the region (such as pushing for recognition of the Fuerzas Armadas Revolucionarias de Colombia [FARC] as a political rather than terrorist organization).

---

[4] Jorge Sapoznikow et al., "Convivencia y Seguridad: Un Reto a la Gobernabilidad," Inter-American Development Bank, 2000.

Recent strains in the U.S.-Latin America relationship, although real, are less a result of alleged U.S. policy failings than a product of deeper changes: while the basic tenets of U.S. policy have not changed, Latin America has. Opening economies, strengthening democracies, and fighting drug production and trafficking remain important priorities. But continuing to build U.S. policy on these pillars alone reflects a mistaken sense of what U.S. policy can realistically achieve and a failure to recognize where Washington can meaningfully bolster Latin Americans' efforts to improve their own quality of life, providing a new foundation for U.S.-Latin America relations in the process. Achieving U.S. objectives and protecting U.S. interests in the Western Hemisphere requires an unsentimental and reality-based assessment of the complex and dynamic changes under way in Latin America and in U.S.-Latin America relations—and of the ways in which the United States can influence those changes for the better.

The Task Force has identified four emerging and urgent priorities that should provide the basis of U.S. policy toward Latin America: 1) poverty and inequality; 2) citizen security; 3) migration; and 4) energy security and integration. These four priorities bear directly on U.S. interests, as their fate will have repercussions on regional stability, democratic consolidation, economic growth and development, and counternarcotics efforts. As important, these four priorities also represent important opportunities for the region and for U.S. policy, opening avenues of dialogue on issues of mutual interest to Latin America and the United States.

Despite the widespread liberalization of Latin American markets and the initiation of targeted development aid programs, nearly 200 million Latin Americans—37 percent of the region's population—still live in poverty, and the region remains one of the most income-unequal in the world. The resulting socioeconomic barriers hinder U.S. interests by spawning political polarization and social turmoil, exposing the vulnerability of already weak state institutions,[5] fueling violence, and hindering economic growth. Poverty and inequality have also undermined support for democracy, as Washington's traditional focus on

---

[5] "Social Panorama of Latin America 2007," Economic Commission for Latin America and the Caribbean (ECLAC), 2007, available at http://www.eclac.org/id.asp?id=30309.

free and fair elections in its democracy promotion efforts has proved insufficient to address fundamental concerns about economic and physical security. Latin America's citizens rightly expect democracy to deliver more equality, social justice, and prosperity—not just formal representation.

Likewise, the focus of U.S. security resources on drug eradication and interdiction has done little to address the underlying factors that drive drug production, trafficking, and consumption. After many years and billions of dollars, U.S. policy has been relatively ineffective in reducing either the supply of or demand for drugs, while public insecurity in Latin America has increased sharply. Crime and violence now rank as two of the most critical threats across much of the region.

The United States cannot solve these problems, but it can help strengthen public institutions and bolster Latin American initiatives to deal with them. U.S. interests will benefit from explicitly recognizing these deep-rooted challenges and working more closely with the private sector, civil society, multilateral institutions, and Latin American governments to address them. *The Task Force finds that strong institutions designed to reduce poverty and inequality and improve citizen security are necessary for Latin American citizens as well as for the realization of core U.S. objectives in the region—democratization, economic growth, and drug control.* While strengthening institutions is first and foremost an issue for Latin American governments to address, the United States can play a role by assisting in targeted ways.

Nearly eighteen million Latin American migrants, legal and illegal, now live in the United States, and the pace of migration—driven largely by the lack of economic opportunity at home—has accelerated in the last twenty years, despite U.S. immigration policies officially designed to thwart it. Substantial percentages of the populations of Mexico and many Central American and Caribbean countries reside and work in the United States; transnational ties formed by individuals and communities constitute de facto U.S.-Latin America integration. The increasing importance of energy resources has further deepened U.S.-Latin America ties, while heightening anxiety over growing "resource nationalism" in countries such as Venezuela, Bolivia, and Ecuador. Latin America already supplies more oil to the United States than does the Middle East, and the region has great potential to be a major provider of alternative fuel sources, increasing U.S. and regional energy security through diversification. *The Task Force finds that the issues of migration and energy security represent not only policy challenges, but also opportunities for the United States and for deepening U.S.-Latin America ties.* The United States can play a positive role in the development of Latin America's traditional and alternative energy markets, enhancing U.S. energy security in the process, while a true reform of immigration policy would bring economic benefits and, through cooperation, enhanced border security for the United States and Latin America alike.

While many policy concerns span the hemisphere, attention to particular bilateral relations is also in order. Although all the countries in Latin America present unique challenges and opportunities, the Task Force focuses on the complex bilateral relations with four nations: Brazil, Mexico, Venezuela, and Cuba. *The Task Force believes that deepening strategic relationships with Brazil and Mexico, and reformulating diplomatic efforts with Venezuela and Cuba, will not only establish more fruitful interactions with these countries but will also positively transform broader U.S.-Latin America relations.*

The realities of poverty and inequality, public security, human mobility, and energy require a more fulsome approach toward Latin America, one that recognizes urgency as well as the primacy of Latin American governments in these efforts. The limits on U.S. policy are equally clear, as these four areas demand concerted efforts by local, state, national, and international governments; the private sector; civil society organizations; and multilateral institutions. As importantly, these issues present real opportunities to engage Latin American countries as partners on problems of mutual concern. This expanded policy framework, combined with greater attention to strategic regional partnerships, will provide a more effective foundation for U.S. policy goals—stability, security, and ultimately prosperity for the United States and for its neighbors.

Poverty and Inequality

Compared to the "lost decade" of the 1980s and the low growth rates of the 1990s, Latin America's economic performance in the early years of the twenty-first century has been strong.[6] The region as a whole grew 5.6 percent in 2007, the fourth consecutive year of growth of more than 4 percent—marking the strongest economic expansion since the 1970s. Panama, Argentina, and Venezuela led with gross domestic product (GDP) growth of 11.2, 8.7, and 8.4 percent, respectively, while several other countries—Colombia, the Dominican Republic, Peru, and Uruguay—grew at 7 percent or more. Even Cuba, according to U.S. estimates, grew at 8 percent, due to high nickel and cobalt prices, as well as tourism.

Other economic indicators have also been positive. Regional inflation was 5.4 percent in 2007, a remarkable achievement given the region's history of hyperinflation. In Peru and Brazil, for example, inflation had gone from more than 3,000 percent in the late 1980s and early 1990s to 1.8 percent and 3.6 percent, respectively, in 2007. Sound fiscal management in many countries has left nearly every government with a strong fiscal position, while Latin America as a whole has a current account surplus of almost 4 percent of GDP. The external debt-to-GDP ratio has also fallen considerably—a function of both

---

[6] The following data, unless otherwise noted, came from the Economic Commission on Latin America and the Caribbean (ECLAC Statistical Yearbook, 2007; ECLAC Social Panorama of Latin America, 2007), the World Bank (World Development Indicators, 2008), and the International Monetary Fund (Western Hemisphere Economic Outlook, April 2008; World Economic Outlook, April 2008).

13

growth and effective economic management—to a regional average of 22 percent of GDP in 2006. The regional poverty rate has declined from 48 percent in the 1990s to 37 percent today, though the number of people living in poverty (due to population growth) is essentially unchanged.

Still, the regional economic picture, although an improvement over the last two decades, leaves much to be desired—particularly when measured against other parts of the developing world. While Latin America grew at an annual average of 2.1 percent between 1995 and 2005, it was outpaced by sub-Saharan Africa (3.8), South Asia (5.8), and East Asia and the Pacific (7).[7] Even the relatively strong 2007 growth rate was topped by sub-Saharan Africa (6.1), South Asia (8.4), and East Asia and the Pacific (10), and the World Bank projects that this disparity will persist in the coming years.[8] Latin America's competitiveness, as measured by the World Bank's "Doing Business" project, also trails its competitors.[9] In the World Economic Forum's "Global Competitiveness Report," only Chile breaks the top 30 out of 131 countries, and Bolivia, Ecuador, Nicaragua, and Paraguay rank near the bottom. China and India stand at 34 and 48, well ahead of Mexico (52), Brazil (72), and Argentina (85).[10]

But more concerning than the overall growth picture is Latin America's slow progress in reducing poverty and inequality. The regional poverty rate of 37 percent is not much lower than the figure for 1980 (40 percent), while the number of poor in Latin America has actually increased, from 136 million in 1980 to nearly 200 million today. (These figures, of course, mask large subregional differences: both Chile and Uruguay have reduced poverty to well under 20 percent, while in Honduras and Nicaragua poverty rates are near 70 percent.) In 1990,

---

[7] "Global Economic Prospects 2008," World Bank, 2008, available at http://siteresources.worldbank.org/INTGEP2008/Resources/complete-report.pdf.

[8] Ibid.

[9] Latin American countries rank on average at 87 among 178 countries in terms of ease of doing business, behind East Asia and the Pacific (77) as well as Eastern Europe and Central Asia (76), although ahead of the Middle East and North Africa (96), South Asia (107), and sub-Saharan Africa (136). "Doing Business 2008," World Bank Group, 2008, available at http://www.doingbusiness.org/.

[10] "The Global Competitiveness Report 2007–2008," World Economic Forum, available at http://www.gcr.weforum.org/.

28 percent of the population in Latin America and the Caribbean lived on less than two dollars a day; by 2005 the rate still stood at 22 percent. East Asia, by contrast, has reduced the percentage of its population living on less than two dollars a day to 29 percent, down from 67 percent in 1990.

Inequality in Latin America, meanwhile, remains extreme. While there have been mild improvements in the Gini coefficient[11] in some countries, the figure for Latin America as a whole is still 0.52—compared to 0.46 for sub-Saharan Africa, 0.41 for the United States, 0.40 for East Asia, and between 0.25 and 0.35 for European nations. In Brazil, the largest country in Latin America, the Gini coefficient is 0.60; the poorest 40 percent of the population accounts for just over 8 percent of national income, while the richest 20 percent accounts for almost 70 percent. Across the region, these figures point to deeper structural realities, such as unequal land distribution and discrimination.

Such extreme and persistent inequality has a variety of negative ramifications for Latin America and the United States—ramifications that, if not addressed, threaten to undermine Latin American governments and U.S. interests in development of the region's broader economic and political stability. Income disparity is closely linked with unequal access to health care, education, and credit and thus, as the World Bank and Inter-American Development Bank have demonstrated, hampers worker productivity, social mobility, and overall growth. While the region has made some progress in terms of health care (infant mortality has fallen by half and life expectancy has increased by six years, to seventy-five, since 1980),[12] the gains have in many cases been concentrated among the better-off portions of the population. In Bolivia, for example, 98 percent of the people in the highest-income quintile have access to health care services, while only 20 percent of those in the lowest quintile do. Previously controlled infectious diseases such as yellow fever, dengue, pertussis, measles, and even the machupo virus are reemerging; the Centers for Disease Control and Prevention

---

[11] Income inequality is often measured by the Gini coefficient, a zero-to-one scale where zero represents perfect income equality (everyone has the same income) and one represents perfect income inequality (a single person has all the country's income).

[12] *The World Bank Annual Report 2007*, World Bank, 2007, available at http://siteresources. worldbank.org/EXTANNREP2K7/Resources/English.pdf.

estimates that some thirteen million people in the region are infected with chagas, an often fatal disease spread by insects.

A vicious cycle of poverty and economic inequality handicaps most Latin American countries, undermining their ability to successfully compete and effectively finance and deliver governmental services, including public security, in an increasingly globalized world. According to a World Bank study, a 10 percent drop in poverty levels can increase growth by 1 percent, while a 10 percent increase in poverty levels can lower growth rate by 1 percent and reduce investment by up to 8 percent of GDP.[13] The effects of ethnic and racial inequity are even stronger: one study has shown that the economies of Bolivia, Brazil, and Guatemala would potentially expand by 37, 13, and 14 percent, respectively, if the long-term social exclusion of Afro-descendant and indigenous groups ended.[14]

Poverty and inequality also have potentially problematic implications for democratic development. With greater democratic representation and regular elections in Latin America, they have become major political issues. Indeed, the widely cited "turn to the left" in the 2005–2007 Latin American elections reflected the economic realities and concerns of the average voter. Growing wage disparity, swelling youth unemployment, weak enforcement of labor protections, and persistent poverty have left some citizens disillusioned with democracy. A survey by Latinobarómetro, a Latin American polling company, of 19,000 individuals in eighteen Latin American countries shows that between 1997 and 2007 those who felt "democracy is preferable to any other kind of government" fell from 63 percent to 54 percent overall. Support for democracy was higher in countries with strong economic performance and lower in countries with weaker economic outcomes. Venezuelans were among the most satisfied with their democracy largely because they felt the government was "addressing their needs." In contrast, Salvadorans had one of the lowest opinions of their current

---

[13] Guillermo E. Perry et al., "Poverty Reduction and Growth: Virtuous and Vicious Cycles," World Bank, 2006, available at http://siteresources.worldbank.org/EXTLACOFFICEOFCE/Resources/870892-1139877599088/virtuous_circles1_complete.pdf.

[14] Jonas Zoninsein, "The Economic Case for Combating Racial and Ethnic Exclusion in Latin American and Caribbean Countries," Inter-American Development Bank, May 2001.

and future economic situation and correspondingly registered both low satisfaction with democracy and low approval of their government.

The Task Force finds that despite positive recent trends, Latin America still lags behind other world regions in its efforts to reduce poverty and income inequality. These barriers represent not only fundamental challenges for Latin American citizens, but they also impede Latin America's economic development, competitiveness, and democratic consolidation. As a result, poverty and inequality also represent fundamental challenges to U.S. objectives in the region. Further progress toward those objectives will require that the United States put underlying economic and political conditions at the center of its policy strategies.

Foreign Policy Efforts: Aid, Trade, and the Fight against Informality

From the 1950s through the 1970s, efforts by international organizations and developed countries to spur development and reduce poverty in poor nations—including much of Latin America—centered on a combination of aid and loans. In the wake of the debt crisis in the 1980s, the approach shifted somewhat to a focus on promoting macroeconomic growth through "structural adjustment" packages. This development strategy—often called the Washington Consensus—promoted market and trade liberalization, as well as specific fiscal policies. Policymakers frequently focused on the benefits of free trade. In the United States, advocates of free trade expected market opening to provide not only benefits for U.S. businesses and consumers but also widespread economic opportunities for Latin America and a reduction of illegal immigration to the United States. President Clinton, for example, argued in 1993 that NAFTA would mean "more disposable income [for Mexicans] to buy more American products, and there will be less illegal immigration because more Mexicans will be able to support their children by staying home."

Since the 1980s, market opening and formal trade agreements between the United States and Latin American countries have increased trade and brought a range of other benefits to both sides. Under NAFTA, trade between the United States, Canada, and Mexico has almost tripled. Mexico has become the United States' third-largest trading partner and the second-largest buyer of U.S. exports, while NAFTA rules and regulations have strengthened intellectual property protection, dispute-resolution mechanisms, and safeguards for labor and environmental standards in Mexico. Newer trade agreements, such as DR-CAFTA and most recently Peru, promise to increase trade and economic opportunities as well.

But all of these measures have had less of an effect on job creation and poverty alleviation than was initially indicated. The opening of Latin American economies, the successful correction of macroeconomic imbalances, and the reform of economic governance structures have not substantially lowered poverty or structural inequality.[15] (Many argue that the fiscal and economic policies of the Washington Consensus have actually heightened inequality in the region, as the enacted policies did not address structural inequalities or micro-level bottlenecks.) Part of the explanation for these shortcomings lies in the maintenance of U.S. government policies—namely, agricultural subsidies and rules-of-origin limits on apparel—that restrict Latin American exports precisely in the areas in which the region has a comparative advantage. At the same time, however, many Latin American governments have not implemented the domestic policies necessary to ensure that the benefits from open markets are more evenly spread. These domestic political and institutional obstacles—in both Washington and Latin America—have had a corrosive effect on support for globalization and trade reform.

At the same time, the nature of employment in Latin America has changed in worrying ways. While official unemployment has fallen in recent years, now averaging roughly 9 percent throughout the region, gains mostly result from growth within the informal labor market. The informal sector includes many self-employed workers—such as artisans, handymen, taxi drivers, and street vendors—as well as informal salaried workers, such as domestic employees, micro-firm workers, and those

---

[15] Brazil may have actually lowered inequality through opening its economy in the 1990s, but it stands alone. See Francisco H.G. Ferreira, Phillippe G. Leite, and Matthew Wai-Poi, "Trade Liberalization, Employment Flows and Wage Inequality in Brazil," World Bank Policy Research Working Paper 4108, January 2007, available at http://www-wds.worldbank.org/servlet/WDSContentServer/WDSP/IB/2007/01/09/000016406_20070109094309/Rendered/PDF/wps4108.pdf.

who work in larger firms under informal labor arrangements. Altogether, it is estimated that about 50 percent of the labor force in the region holds informal sector jobs. (National figures range from 32 percent in Chile and 43 percent in Mexico to more than 60 percent in Bolivia, Ecuador, Nicaragua, and Paraguay.) Informal employment has offered some workers—particularly women and low-skilled workers in general—a way to create wealth and to alleviate extreme poverty.[16] But informal salaried workers earn less, averaging between 40 and 66 percent of formal salaried employees, and the spread of informality has limited the state's capacity to provide basic services by removing much of the economy from the tax system. It leaves, as a consequence, a substantial proportion of workers without access to social safety-net programs or health care. For the poor—those more likely to be in the informal sector—this limits opportunities and productivity in the longer term.

The Task Force finds that trade—which has spurred regional growth—and development aid have not and cannot alone lead to sufficient reductions in poverty and economic inequality in Latin America. The growth of the informal sector, while often successful in increasing incomes for the poor, undermines the economic base of Latin American countries and the effectiveness of state institutions, which are critical in addressing the region's fundamental challenges.

Latin American Solutions to Latin America's Problems

Some countries have broken out of the cycle of poverty. The most notable example is Chile, which has averaged 5.6 percent growth since 1990. It has also benefited from a strong and lasting commitment to consistent macroeconomic policies, open markets, expanded social programs, and institutional strengthening, broadly shared across the political spectrum, since its transition to democracy in 1990. Chile has reduced its poverty levels from over 40 percent in the late 1980s to around 14 percent in 2006 (nearly equal to U.S. rates). The absolute number of citizens considered poor fell from close to five million in the late 1980s to just over two million at the end of 2006. Chile has

---

[16] "Poverty and the Informal Sector," United Nations Economic and Social Council, October 2, 2006, available at http://www.unescap.org/pdd/CPR/CPR2006/English/CPR3_1E.pdf.

been less successful at reducing its high rate of income inequality, though this too has fallen slightly during the last few years.

Other Latin American experiences show that poverty and inequality reductions are not wholly dependent on uninterrupted economic growth. Brazil, for example, has reduced poverty and inequality during the last two decades despite the absence of consistent strong growth: by controlling inflation, it managed to lower poverty rates from a 1990 high of 48 percent to 36 percent by 1996. Though poverty levels crept back up to 39 percent in the early 2000s, modest economic growth combined with conditional cash transfer programs in recent years have helped reduce poverty to 33 percent by 2006. Brazil has also managed to begin lowering its notoriously high levels of income inequality in recent years. In Mexico, similar cash transfers, along with low inflation, helped reduce poverty levels from 47 percent in 1990 to 32 percent in 2006.

These achievements represent domestic policy efforts—under civilian democratic governments—to address critical concerns of the voting population and indicate real improvements in the lives of millions of citizens throughout Latin America. These experiences show that domestic solutions, sometimes drawing on foreign models adapted to the local environment, can be effective. Conditional cash transfer programs have spread across the region, including Oportunidades in Mexico (which was recently cited by Mayor Michael Bloomberg as a model for a pilot program in New York City), Famílias en Acción in Colombia, and Bolsa Família in Brazil. Such programs provide cash subsidies for the poor in return for a combination of regular school attendance by their children and use of preventive medical care. Evidence shows that these programs are instrumental in reducing poverty and increasing primary and secondary school attendance, at least in the short term.[17]

Another promising development is the spread of microfinance. Latin Americans have historically suffered from unequal access to financial

---

[17] Some question whether these gains are sustainable in the longer term, since they do not normally focus on job creation or address the quality of education. See Fernando Reimers et al., "Where is the 'Education' in Conditional Cash Transfers in Education?" UNESCO Institute for Statistics, Montreal, 2006.

services. Only 14.5 percent of poor households in Latin America and the Caribbean have a savings account and just over 3 percent have access to credit from formal or semiformal financial institutions,[18] limiting the ability of the poor to accumulate assets, efficiently manage risk, or leverage their entrepreneurial skills and abilities. The growth in micro- and small-enterprise financing from private aid organizations, local and international governments, international institutions, and private capital markets has begun to reduce this discrimination and foster job creation. Latin America's microfinance banks currently have four million to five million clients. Although access is expanding, its availability must be accelerated to support a significant portion of the estimated fifty million microenterprises in Latin America.

Individuals and families in Latin America—rather than governments or aid organizations—have adopted another "solution" to poverty: migration. As detailed below, migration within the Western Hemi- sphere has exploded in the last twenty years. While populations and countries depend on the "pull" of employment, continued poverty and lack of economic opportunity have "pushed" many to search for work abroad, whether in neighboring countries, Europe, or the United States. Migration has reduced pressure on the receiving local job market while often providing stable income flows (in the form of remittances) to the family members who stay behind. These funds are injected into local economies through basic household spending, as well as at times through investment in local businesses and real estate.

While many Latin American governments are dedicated to fighting poverty and inequality, substantial barriers remain. The lack of adequate credit and property registries, banking facilities, and industry regulations hinders financial access. While credit registries have existed for a long time in Latin America, they often lack the information necessary to analyze the credit records of potential customers. In many countries, property registries are not well maintained, making it hard for the population to use property as collateral. There is also a lack of banking

---

[18] Luis Tejerina et al., "Financial Services and Poverty Reduction in Latin America and the Caribbean," Inter-American Development Bank, 2006, available at http://www.iadb.org/ sds/doc/POV-FSPovertyReduction.pdf.

presence in rural areas and a lack of financial literacy among the populations that could most benefit from financial access. Finally, financial regulations often exclude micro-lending and discourage the expansion of private capital (alongside government and nongovernmental organization [NGO] money) for small loans.

Underlying these challenges is a general lack of public resources in Latin America. The regressive nature of Latin America's tax systems and the informality of large sectors of the economy often mean that the state simply lacks the money for effective antipoverty policies. Latin American tax systems rely mostly on value-added taxes (VAT) rather than mixes of personal, property, and corporate income taxes. Furthermore, while collection rates vary, Latin American governments on average collect just 17 percent of GDP in taxes, compared to the Organization for Economic Cooperation and Development (OECD) levels of 35 percent.[19]

The Task Force finds that addressing high rates of poverty and inequality represents a critical challenge for governments in the region, one in which the U.S. government, nonprofit organizations, and multilateral institutions can play a supporting role. There are currently several hopeful "homegrown" policy examples, including conditional cash transfers and microenterprise and small-business loans, but the expansion of these programs and the creation of an effective social safety net will depend both on increasing public resources and enhancing state capacity.

U.S. Policy Today

Throughout the 1990s, trade and market opening generally dominated the U.S.-Latin America agenda. While increased openness has enhanced aggregate growth, specific programs targeting poverty remain critical. Unfortunately, poverty-oriented aid to the region, administered by the U.S. Agency for International Development (USAID), has remained fixed at an annual $600 million for the entire region for the last decade,

---

[19] Brazil is an exception, with tax collection nearing 40 percent of income. Unfortunately, for the issues of concern here, most of its social expenditure is earmarked regressively, for middle- and upper-class programs such as public pensions. "Latin America Economic Outlook 2008," OECD, 2008, available at http://www.oecd.org/dataoecd/61/44/39563883.pdf.

putting it at roughly one-third of 1980 levels in real terms. (To put this amount in perspective, it should be pointed out that the Mexican and Brazilian governments each spend over $2.5 billion per year on flagship social programs.) This decline is especially notable given the increase in funding for other initiatives, most notably those related to counternarcotics, which now receive some $1.2 billion per year (mostly for drug eradication and interdiction).

The Millennium Challenge Account (MCA), President Bush's plan for increased development assistance, does not make up for these short-comings. Since MCA grants are targeted at the very poorest nations, only seven Latin American countries qualify: agreements have been signed with Nicaragua, Honduras, Paraguay, and El Salvador, and Guyana, Paraguay, and Peru are receiving funds as part of the MCA's Threshold Program. But the structure of the MCA leaves millions of desperately poor communities, particularly in larger countries such as Brazil and Mexico, ineligible.

In 2007, the Bush administration expressed fresh concern about Latin America's socioeconomic conditions, partly in response to the perceived challenge of leaders such as President Chávez. It began to emphasize the United States' interest in "social justice" in its public pronouncements when meeting with Latin American leaders and sent the USS *Comfort* on a four-month tour of twelve nations in Latin America and the Caribbean to provide primary medical services and assistance. President Bush announced a health care professional training center in Panama that will serve all of Central America, along with some credit support for small- and medium-sized businesses. Unfortu-nately, the United States has not followed up with a large commitment of new resources to other Latin American countries, in sharp contrast to the nearly $9 billion that Venezuela pledged in 2007 for financing, energy funding, and welfare programs.[20]

The Task Force finds that the issues of persistent poverty and income inequality must be better targeted by U.S. policymakers beyond the largely

---

[20] The nearly $9 billion figure comes from Natalie Obiko Pearson and Ian James, "Chávez Offers Billions in Latin America," Associated Press, August 26, 2007. It includes $1 billion worth of Argentine bonds that Venezuela pledged to buy in 2007, but does not include another $4 billion of Argentine bonds that Venezuela claims to have bought in the past two years.

traditional reliance on trade and democratization alone. A failure to recognize and target these issues better will undercut broader U.S. policy objectives.

Public Security

Latin America presents an odd paradox: while it is one of the most peaceful regions in the world in terms of cross-border violence, non-state violence in various forms is both prevalent and serious. The World Health Organization (WHO) ranks Latin America as the world's most violent region, with a homicide rate three times the global average. Most of the region's politically motivated civil conflicts, the scourge of many Latin American societies from the 1960s into the 1990s, are over or in the process of winding down. But other forms of violence—ranging from that generated by drug trafficking organizations and trans-national criminal cartels to petty local crime rings and gangs—have spread alarmingly, defying predictions that economic growth and an aging population would ameliorate such problems.

According to Latinobarómetro, 17 percent of all Latin Americans rate the lack of personal security as one of the most important problems in their society (second only to unemployment), a figure that nearly doubled between 2003 and 2006. In many countries—including Brazil, Colombia, El Salvador, Guatemala, and Venezuela—personal security ranks as the most direct challenge facing society. According to a study jointly conducted by the IDB and universities in six Latin American countries, rates of violent crime and crimes against property are now six times higher in Latin America than in the rest of the world. More than four of every ten people killed by gunfire globally are killed in Latin America, even though the region accounts for less than 10 percent of the world population.

Aside from the human toll, the economic cost of violence is staggering. Measures of direct and indirect economic impact vary, but IDB studies have put it at the equivalent of 14 percent of total GDP in Latin America. The World Bank's *World Development Report* has noted that 50 percent of businesses surveyed in Latin America said crime was a serious obstacle to their ability to do business. The IDB has concluded, "Violence is without a doubt the principal limit to economic development in Latin America."

In short, public insecurity could undermine progress on a variety of other fronts if not addressed urgently and adequately. As the vice president of Colombia, Francisco Santos, recently stated, "Crime is the biggest problem of the next decade. It will hinder tourism, investment, and threaten democracy."[21] It is also a challenge that weighs heavily on the region's relationship with the United States. Drug production and trafficking have long been among the defining issues of U.S.-Latin America relations. More recently, given economic ties and continuing migratory flows, the threat represented by transnational gangs has highlighted a deepening connection between the United States and Latin American security.

Ultimately, the problem of public security lies at the intersection of a number of other problems in Latin America: poverty, economic discrimination, weak rule of law, corruption and impunity, and migratory trends.[22] Addressing crime and personal security is thus crucial for the region's growth and stability.

Worrying Trends, Vicious Cycles

For many years, Colombia was the country most affected by violence in Latin America. The armed conflict in Colombia had political origins, but it long ago morphed into something driven far more by the drug trade than by ideology, engulfing the country in a swirl of criminal and insurgent violence that made it one of the most dangerous countries

---

[21] Andrew Bounds, "Violent crime called 'biggest threat' to Latin America," *Financial Times*, September 19, 2006.

[22] "Outsiders? The Changing Patterns of Exclusion in Latin America and the Caribbean 2008," The Economic and Social Progress Report, Inter-American Development Bank, 2007.

in the world. In the past five years, however, murder rates have fallen by more than a third nationally, and even more in the country's major cities of Bogotá, Medellín, and Cali, while kidnapping has been reduced by about 80 percent. The state is now present in many regions previously controlled by illegal armed groups, reestablishing elected governments, building and rebuilding public infrastructure, and affirming the rule of law. The October 2007 regional elections were the least violent in the past ten years. These substantial improvements are due to concerted efforts by the Colombian government, with assistance from the United States through Plan Colombia. Colombia still has very serious security problems and neither left-wing insurgency nor right-wing paramilitary forces (both drug-fueled and extremely violent) have been eliminated, but important progress has been made.

A good portion of the rest of the region has either seen an increase in violence or is stuck at an unacceptably high level of violence. There is, of course, significant variation throughout Latin America. In the Andes and parts of Central America, for example, the murder rate is above forty per 100,000 people; in the Southern Cone, outside of Brazil, it is under ten (as compared to one per 100,000 people in industrialized countries). A handful of countries, notably Chile, Uruguay, and Costa Rica, have levels of crime and violence comparable to developed countries.

In Central America the increasing prevalence of violence is a cause of serious concern, even as the civil wars that plagued the region into the 1990s have ended. Homicide rates in Guatemala and El Salvador are higher today than they were during those countries' civil wars; according to government statistics, the murder rate has doubled in Guatemala since 1999. The executive director of the UN Office on Drugs and Crime recently summed up the variety and magnitude of Central America's security challenges: "Where crime and corruption reign and drug money perverts the economy, the State no longer has a monopoly on the use of force and citizens no longer trust their leaders and public institutions." Three other countries also exhibit worrisome trends: Brazil, Mexico, and Venezuela. High levels of drug violence plague both Brazil and Mexico, with drug gangs in Brazilian cities and traffickers throughout northern Mexico threatening government control in many areas. In Brazil in 2007, a battle between drug gangs and police in São Paulo turned the city into a war zone for days, leaving scores dead. That same year in Mexico, more than 2,500 people were killed in drug violence. Urban crime in Venezuela has also increased significantly in recent years; by some measures, Caracas has become the most dangerous city in Latin America.

The prevalence of non-state violence underscores the fact that some states cannot effectively control or govern their national territory. This includes not only remote areas such as southern and eastern Colombia and the Brazilian Amazon, but also some poor areas of Latin America's megacities, including the *favelas* of Rio de Janeiro or the *ranchos* of Caracas, where the government often fails to provide the most basic law enforcement and judicial services. The increasing privatization of security, in many places, has exacerbated this already weak state capacity, encouraging citizens to put their trust in gated communities and private security providers instead of the state's police and judicial systems. There are, by some measures, more than half a million private security personnel in Latin America today.

These problems reflect the state's fundamental inability to maintain a monopoly over the use of force and to satisfy the basic social contract with their citizens. This is a consequence, to some degree, of Latin America's economic inequality and widespread social exclusion: with limited opportunities for education and legal economic advancement, youths are more likely to take up lives of crime. Weak state capacity is also in evidence: local and national governments, often underfunded, poorly administered, and plagued by corruption, have little capacity to control the streets of the cities and to prevent powerful criminal networks from taking hold.

The degree of impunity is also alarming. A study by a prominent Mexican research center found that 96 percent of crimes go unpunished in Mexico, while officials believe that 75 percent of crimes are not even reported. In Brazil, less than 10 percent of murderers are convicted. Polling consistently shows that between a quarter and half of Latin Americans have very little trust in the police and judicial systems, which leads to significant underreporting of crime, thereby contributing to impunity and encouraging the kinds of vigilantism and paramilitarism that exacerbate the original problem. In many countries, citizens view the police as part of the problem, rather than part of the solution. This is a result, in part, of underfunding and poor management, as well as of corruption and abuses of power by law enforcement. According to Latinobarómetro, in 2007, 19 percent of Latin Americans reported that in the past twelve months either they or someone in their family had witnessed an act of corruption. The Global Corruption Barometer, a survey conducted by Transparency International, consistently finds that as many as 10 percent of Latin Americans have paid bribes in the past month and ranks most Latin American countries in the bottom half of its corruption perceptions index.

The prison systems of many Latin American countries further exacerbate the security problem. In many countries, prisons are notoriously overcrowded, make little effort at rehabilitation, and are controlled by gangs—turning petty criminals into more violent offenders who often become part of large national and even transnational criminal networks. Other concerns include public support for extralegal responses, including coercive law enforcement and interrogation techniques, vigilante justice in countries such as Haiti, Guatemala, Peru, and Bolivia, and continued paramilitarism in Colombia and Brazil.

The Task Force finds that many Latin American countries, including Brazil, Mexico, Venezuela, and most Central American nations, are caught in a vicious cycle in which corruption and weak state capacity—particularly in law enforcement and judicial institutions—help to drive violence and crime. This dynamic also threatens U.S. policy interests in reducing drug trafficking and promoting stability in the region.

Transnational Threats

A variety of transnational threats have flourished under these conditions, and a number of them are of particular concern to the United States: drugs, international criminal cartels, gangs, and terrorism.

Drugs

A considerable amount of violence in Latin America is directly or indirectly related to the drug trade. Given the amount of illicit money involved relative to the size of the legal economies in the region, it is no surprise that the drug trade has a powerful capacity to undercut the state. According to the UN Office on Drugs and Crime's 2007 "World Drug Report," Latin America produces nearly one thousand metric tons of cocaine every year, supplying the U.S. market with drugs worth more than $60 billion, as well as significant amounts of heroin, marijuana, and methamphetamine. The sheer size of the drug trade has had a massive effect on the security situation in every country involved, especially Bolivia, Colombia, and Peru, the three primary drug-producing countries; and Brazil, the Caribbean, Central America, Mexico, and Venezuela, all of which are part of trafficking routes (and plagued by increasing drug consumption as well). Because so much of a drug's added value accrues during the smuggling phase, trafficking is just as likely as production to cause violence in a country.

The stated purpose of the $5 billion aid package known as Plan Colombia was to support counternarcotics efforts in Colombia, which, it was estimated at the time, supplied some 90 percent of the world's cocaine and a significant portion of the heroin that arrives in the United States. This assistance has been indispensable in contributing to the strengthening of state institutions in Colombia. These improvements have been critical in ensuring the Colombian state's ability to improve public security for its citizens through policing power.

While the public security gains are indisputable, it is also the case that Plan Colombia has not stemmed drug flows into the United States. Prices for cocaine and heroin are as low as or lower than ever. In the case of cocaine, the street price of a gram is, according to both UN and U.S. government data, around a third of what it was in the 1980s, before Washington devoted billions of dollars to the war on drugs, and purity is higher. Additionally, despite a considerable amount of aerial spraying of coca crops and record seizures of cocaine, drug production in the Andean region has stabilized at roughly one thousand metric tons. Reductions in supply from Colombia in the last few years have been accompanied by increases in production in Peru and Bolivia.[23]

---

[23] "World Drug Report 2007," United Nations Office on Drugs and Crime, 2007, available at http://www.unodc.org/pdf/research/wdr07/WDR_2007.pdf.

As drug violence in Colombia has declined, it has increased significantly in Mexico. This has resulted, in part, from Mexico's growing importance as a trafficking route and increasing competition among different trafficking organizations. It has also resulted from expanded drug production in Mexico, where producers create synthetic drugs such as methamphetamine that are then trafficked to the United States. Mexico's own security forces have proved unable or unwilling to take on the well-funded and well-armed Mexican cartels, and in many cases have been corrupted by those cartels. President Felipe Calderón has made confronting the drug problem one of his administration's major objectives (and turned the task over to the military, in acknowledgment that Mexico's police have been unable to make much headway), with promises of considerable financial and technical assistance from Washington. While the immediate result of Calderón's tactics has been more frequent interdiction, it remains unclear whether his administration will prove more able than his predecessor's in controlling the problem, especially given the value of drug profits that flow into the cartels' hands.

Security assistance to Mexico this decade has been inadequate. While Colombia received over $500 million each year from 2000–2007, Mexico received less than $40 million annually. The Merida Initiative proposed by the Bush administration in October 2007 addresses this issue by proposing a $1.4 billion assistance program over the next three years (which includes modest sums that would go to Central America). While the initiative recognizes the need for greater investment in promoting rule of law and security on both sides of the border, its initial focus on hardware means that it may not do enough on the more important issue of institution-building and strengthening, an important success of Plan Colombia.

Drug consumption, long viewed as confined to the United States, has also been on the rise in many Latin American countries, creating an increasingly worrisome public health problem, as well as contributing to an upsurge in both petty and more serious crime. Cocaine consumption has also expanded in Europe. Of the one thousand metric tons produced each year in the region, slightly more than half is now bound for areas other than North America.

U.S. policy focuses primarily on eradication and interdiction in the source countries, but studies show that growers in producing countries respond rapidly to U.S. pressure by growing more than the market demands, knowing that some of their product will be destroyed or seized. Since substantial value added to illegal drugs is in trafficking, losing a percentage of the product early in the process does not imply significant economic loss for drug cartels. It is estimated that every dollar put into domestic U.S. enforcement is three times more effective in reducing U.S. consumption than a similar investment in decreasing production in the source country. This is particularly true for newly popular drugs with expanding markets, such as methamphetamine. For drugs with more "mature markets"—such as cocaine—domestic enforcement is not as useful, as dealers are rapidly replaced and addicts are generally willing to pay any price to satisfy their addiction. Treatment and rehabilitation are more cost-effective than either domestic law enforcement or source country eradication and interdiction.[24]

The Task Force finds that the drug trade flourishes from a volatile combination of negative socioeconomic conditions in producing and trafficking countries coupled with high demand for narcotics in the United States and Europe, and increasingly in Latin America itself. Effectively fighting the drug trade will require not only supply eradication and interdiction efforts, but also policies in Latin America that address underlying conditions and weak governance that allows the trade to thrive. As important, U.S. and European policies must target the demand for drugs in their countries, which create markets lucrative enough to overwhelm even well-funded and well-designed security and eradication efforts.

New Threats to the United States? Gangs and Terrorism

Much of the recent interest about transnational threats in Latin America stems from concerns that the region may serve as a base or breeding ground for terrorist organizations. This fear was highlighted when some of the people involved in an incipient terrorist plot at John F. Kennedy airport in New York were found to have come from Guyana and Trinidad and Tobago. Attention has also focused on the triborder area where Argentina, Brazil, and Paraguay meet, which is home to

---

[24] Jonathan P. Caulkins, "How Goes the 'War on Drugs'?: An Assessment of U.S. Drug Problems and Policy," RAND Drug Policy Research Center, 2005, available at http://www.rand.org/pubs/occasional_papers/2005/RAND_OP121.pdf.

considerable criminal activity and relatively low levels of government control. There is some evidence that Hezbollah has had a limited presence in the area for purposes of money laundering, but there is no strong evidence thus far that Middle East terrorist operatives have had much success making inroads into Latin America. Similarly, although Hugo Chávez's ties with Iran and provocative statements about the United States have raised concern in many quarters, there is little evidence that Venezuela currently presents a haven for Islamic terrorism. Nonetheless, as Admiral Stavridis, Commander of the U.S. Southern Command, expressed to Congress earlier this year, while narcoterrorism (addressed below) is a constant struggle for the region, "Islamic radical terrorism is a much less immediate force in the region, but it has the potential to become of greater concern to us."

More immediately relevant are transnational gangs that have been flagged as a serious emerging threat to hemispheric security. The two most prominent and dangerous gangs, the M-18 and the MS-13, have somewhere between 50,000 and 100,000 members distributed among a number of Central American countries (especially Guatemala, El Salvador, and Honduras) and the United States. The Congressional Research Service recently reported that more than 1,300 members of the MS-13 have been arrested in the United States in the past two and a half years. By many accounts, the origin of transnational gangs stemmed from the release of tens of thousands of criminals, deported from the United States to Central American nations, where often the receiving governments were uninformed of the criminal background of the deportees, leaving their judicial and prison systems unable to control them.

State agencies in Central America and the United States have made a concerted effort to understand and address the threat. In 2004 the FBI created a special task force on gangs, which works with Central American governments. The State Department, Department of Homeland Security (DHS), the U.S. Agency for International Development, and the Department of Justice have also developed initiatives that support and work with Central American governments on gang-related issues and threats. The IDB and USAID have funded a variety of youth and educational programs in an effort to dissuade Central American youth from gang involvement. There have also been meetings between local law enforcement officials in the United States and their Central American counterparts to facilitate coordination and information sharing.

The threat posed by transnational gangs should not be overstated, as it has been in some of the more tendentious analyses of the problem in recent years. The UN Office on Drugs and Crime has found that, while gangs in Central America "represent a source of criminality, they do not appear to be responsible for a particularly disproportionate share of the murders in the countries where they predominate. Their role in drug trafficking . . . is also dubious."[25] Still, the gangs do contribute to already high rates of crime and further undermine weak governance in several Central American countries; if not met with effective anticrime strategies in Latin America and continued coordination between Central American governments and the United States, such gangs could become an increasingly problematic threat to security and stability.

The Task Force finds that the United States must be vigilant toward emerging threats without letting them hamper U.S. policy in other critical areas. In addition, claims that terrorists are using Latin America as a launching pad for attack on the United States are thus far unfounded.

Cross-border Threats

Cross-border threats among countries of the region are much diminished today, thanks to the end of military governments in the region, relatively low levels of defense spending, few significant external threats, the settling or tabling of most major border disputes, the influence of the United States and other members of the international community, and improving mechanisms for regional cooperation through the OAS and other regional and subregional bodies. Of concern, however, are Venezuela's international arms purchases, which increased from an estimated $71 million between 2002 and 2004 to $4 billion between 2005 and 2007, expenditures not included in the country's official

---

[25] "Crime and Development in Central America: Caught in the Crossfire," United Nations Office on Drugs and Crime, May 2007.

military budget.[26] While aggregate defense expenditures in Latin America remain among the lowest regionally in the world as a percentage of GDP, such substantial Venezuelan increases should be watched.

In addition, the March 2008 crisis following a Colombian strike on a camp belonging to the terrorist group FARC in Ecuadorian territory—which killed Raúl Reyes, the FARC's second-in-command—indicates the persistence of destabilizing forces in the region. The Colombian government described the strike as self-defense; President Chávez, President Correa, and several other heads of state rushed to condemn Colombia's actions. In what soon became the tensest diplomatic crisis the Andes had experienced in decades, Ecuador cut relations with Colombia, and both Ecuador and Venezuela expelled the Colombian ambassadors from their capitals and mobilized their armed forces to the Colombian border.

Peaceful resolution of the crisis at the Rio Summit in the Dominican Republic showed, on the one hand, the importance of institutional and legal mechanisms for security cooperation and dispute resolution, especially those under the OAS. But as a general matter such mechanisms remain weak, and improving and deepening them will be critical to averting such crises in the future. Other forums for regional and subregional cooperation, though not specifically dedicated to security cooperation (such as Mercosur and the Community of Andean Nations), have been beneficial in reducing and managing interstate tensions. Other proposed or incipient security forums, such as the South American Defense Council and the Ameripol regional police force, could also play a positive role. Signed in 1967, the Treaty of Tlatelolco has, so far, succeeded in committing the entire Latin American region to remain free of nuclear weapons. While these mechanisms, taken together, do not provide an especially robust regional system for managing interstate conflict, they do comprise a system of norms and practices aimed at resolving such disputes—and offer a platform on which to build.

While Colombia's cross-border raid led to a regional diplomatic crisis, it also brought to the surface the concerns of many of the region's

---

[26] "The List: The World's Biggest Military Buildups," *Foreign Policy*, November 2007, available at http://www.foreignpolicy.com/story/cms.php?story_id=4051.

governments apart from Colombia—including Argentina, Brazil, Mexico, Panama, and Peru—over the persistence of the FARC and possible efforts by regional actors to abet and prolong the FARC's destabilizing presence. The Colombian government has alleged that it found three laptop computers at the site where Reyes was killed that contained evidence of support for the FARC by the Venezuelan and Ecuadorian governments. The alleged support included a $300 million fund that Chávez's government was going to set up for the FARC and acceptance by the Ecuadorian government of the FARC's presence in Ecuadorian territory. If authenticated by Interpol, the information obtained from several hard drives in the coming months may substantiate allegations of deliberate support by Venezuela for the FARC, which the United States, the European Union, and Canada consider a terrorist organization. The Colombian government also found thirty kilograms of depleted uranium near Bogotá that it claims were going to be delivered to the FARC, raising fears that the FARC has an interest in obtaining nuclear material.

Even as the Colombian Armed Forces continue to weaken the FARC militarily and psychologically, the incident exposed the FARC's continuing pursuit of international ties and highlighted the need for greater regional cooperation to put an end to the region's longest-standing insurgent group. *The Task Force finds that the regional dimensions of the Colombian conflict remain significant and require greater discipline and cooperation among Latin American countries in order to successfully tackle the shared challenge posed by violent criminal syndicates and insurgent groups that thrive on weak institutions and contraband to destabilize governments in the region.*

Also troublesome is the vast number of mostly unregistered guns in the region. In Central America, estimates range from two million to four million (many left over from earlier civil wars and conflicts), with less than 800,000 registered with the government. The United States is another important source of illegal firearms and sophisticated weaponry. Over 10 percent of U.S. gun shops are located near the Mexican border and these businesses sell on average twice the number of arms than their counterparts more distant from the border.

Smuggling guns into Mexico, a country with strict gun laws, can be a profitable venture: an AK-47 worth $500 in the United States can be sold for as much as $1,500 in Mexico.[27] While Mexico has only 6,000 legally registered guns in the country, every year the government confiscates between 5,000 and 10,000 illegal firearms, more than 90 percent of which are traced to the United States. Between January and October 2007 the Mexican government seized 6,000 weapons, 470 grenades, and 552,000 rounds of ammunition.[28] Reflecting the plentiful supply of guns in the country, criminals have recently been leaving their weapons at the crime scene.

International drug trafficking organizations derive their power not only from powerful weapons, but also from drug money coming from the United States and other consuming countries. The Drug Enforcement Administration (DEA) estimates that Mexican and Colombian drug trafficking organizations launder between $8 billion and $25 billion every year. Much of this comes from sales throughout the United States, where profits are transferred to border towns (predominantly through wire transfers) and then transported out of the country, usually through bulk cash smuggling across the southern border. Once the money is in Mexico, it is stashed for future financing of international criminal organizations, moved further south, deposited in currency exchange houses or banks, or transported back to the United States via armored car or courier service. This sophisticated smuggling system allows criminal organizations to claim the funds as legitimate deposits in banks and makes it hard to trace the funds to drug trafficking. The Mexican attorney general estimates that approximately $10 billion of laundered Mexican drug money ends up in U.S. banks every year.

These laundered funds and smuggled weapons sustain and reinforce the power of international criminal organizations, assisting them in compromising or overwhelming Latin American governments. *The Task Force finds that transnational crime is aided by the widespread availability of handguns and small arms, and ready funding from the lucrative drug trade.*

---

[27] Sam Logan, "Guns: The Bloody U.S.-Mexico Market," ISN Security Watch, October 31, 2007, available at http://www.isn.ethz.ch/news/sw/details.cfm?id = 18300.

[28] Manuel Roig-Franzia, "U.S. Guns Behind Cartel Killings in Mexico," *Washington Post*, October 29, 2007, available at http://www.washingtonpost.com/wp-dyn/content/article/2007/10/28/AR2007102801654.html.

Regional cooperation is critical for effective responses, as illegal non-state organizations and criminal networks do not operate within or respect national or international borders.

Integration through Migration

Over one hundred million Latin Americans have left their homes since World War II. While three-quarters of Latin American migrants today move to the United States, there is also significant migration to other regions and within Latin America itself. The volume of such movement has been a primary force in the integration of the Western Hemisphere in recent decades, reshaping economies and societies in the process. Public policy has failed to keep up.

About forty-five million Latinos currently live in the United States, eighteen million of them foreign born.[29] Central Americans and Mexicans make up 71 percent of this total; people from the Caribbean (mostly from the Dominican Republic, Haiti, and Cuba) 18 percent; and South Americans (primarily from Colombia, Ecuador, and Peru) 11 percent. In some cases, this represents a sizable portion of the sending country's population: the eleven million Mexicans in the United States, for example, comprise roughly 10 percent of Mexico's population and 15 percent of its labor force. El Salvador, Guatemala, and Honduras have one million, 750,000, and 400,000 of their respective nationals living in the United States, representing 35 percent, 19 percent, and 15 percent of their respective labor forces.[30]

---

[29] For the purposes of this report, the term Latinos will be used to refer to both Latin Americans and their descendants living in the United States.

[30] El Salvador's labor force is 2.865 million, Guatemala's is 3.958 million, and Honduras's is 2.489 million. The World Factbook 2008, Central Intelligence Agency, available at https://www.cia.gov/library/publications/the-world-factbook/index.html.

The U.S. workforce, meanwhile, has become increasingly dependent on these workers. Between mid-2005 and mid-2006, Latinos accounted for 37 percent of the total increase in workers in the United States. They now account for around 13 percent of the U.S. labor force, and more than a quarter of the labor force in states such as Arizona.[31] They represent 41 percent of total employment in farming, fishing, and forestry, 25 percent in the construction sector, and 28 percent in cleaning and maintenance.[32] While legal migrants are evenly split between males and females, some 60 percent of illegal migrants are men. These workers tend to be poorer and less educated than native-born American workers or migrants from other regions. Seventy-nine percent of Asian migrants and 87 percent of African immigrants over age twenty-five have completed high school, compared to only 44 percent of Latin American migrants over age twenty-five. As a result, Latin American migrants generally enter into lower-skilled sectors of the U.S. economy. Although the issue is much debated, most analysts find the net economic impact of immigrants on the U.S. economy modestly positive. The U.S. Council of Economic Advisers has found that immigrants "have an overall positive effect on the income of native-born workers,"[33] largely because immigrants, when arrayed by years of schooling, are concentrated at the extremes of the education ladder, complementing U.S. workers who are grouped in the middle of the spectrum.

Migration within Latin America is also significant and accelerating. Official statistics put the number of Latin Americans living outside of their home countries but within the region at five million, but considerable evidence suggests that the real number is much higher, as porous borders, informal economies, and understaffed bureaucracies make tracking difficult. Argentina, Costa Rica, and Venezuela are the primary destinations. Argentina is home to significant numbers of Bolivians,

---

[31] "Arizona: Population and Labor Force Characteristics 2000-2006," Pew Hispanic Center, January 23, 2008, available at http://pewhispanic.org/files/factsheets/37.pdf.

[32] Ibid. and Rakesh Kochhar, "Latino Labor Report, 2006: Strong Gains in Employment," Pew Hispanic Center, September 27, 2006, available at http://pewhispanic.org/files/reports/70.pdf.

[33] "Immigration's Economic Impact," Council of Economic Advisers, June 20, 2007, available at http://www.whitehouse.gov/cea/cea_immigration_062007.pdf.

Chileans, and Paraguayans; Costa Rica to as many as 500,000 Nicaraguans; and Venezuela to several hundred thousand Colombians. Bolivia, in contrast, has lost some two million people—20 percent of its population—to migration in recent years. Recent evidence also suggests that the composition of such migration within Latin America is changing, with a growing portion of skilled migrants leaving for other countries in the region. Around half of migrants to Chile, Mexico, and Panama have twelve or more years of schooling.

In prior decades Latin Americans often migrated in response to political upheaval or violent conflict. Today, migration is mostly driven by economics. The U.S. minimum wage, at close to seven dollars per hour, is six to seven times that of Mexico's, which is, in turn, higher than that of most of Central America. U.S. per capita GDP is over $43,000, compared to Mexico's $11,000, El Salvador's $5,500, and Guatemala's $4,300. There is also great demand for Latin American immigrant workers in the United States: the foreign-born Latino unemployment rate in the second quarter of 2006 was 3.9 percent, identical to that for non-Latino white population born in the United States.[34] The same dynamic holds for migration within Latin America: Costa Rica's GDP, for example, is more than four times that of Nicaragua, helping to account for the numbers of Nicaraguans working in Costa Rica. One additional factor in determining migration patterns is existing networks of migrants: established family or community ties from previous waves of migration arrange housing, employment, and general support and thereby facilitate continued flows even when economic incentives decline.

The Task Force finds that demographic trends, economic opportunity, and established immigrant networks are the primary causes of current migratory trends, encouraging men and women to search for better opportunities abroad. As long as these underlying factors hold, substantial migration within the region and from the region to the United States will continue, even in the face of restrictive immigration policies.

---

[34] Ibid.

Remittances and Circular Migration: Economic Development Tools?

Remittances have become a critical source of income for many developing countries. In 2007, over $66.5 billion was remitted to Latin America and the Caribbean, about three-quarters of which came from the United States.[35] This is equal to 80 percent of all foreign direct investment in the region. Mexico received the largest cross-border flows—approximately $24 billion—while remittances to El Salvador and Honduras exceeded 20 percent of national income. In the United States, 73 percent of adult Latin American immigrants—some thirteen million people—regularly send remittances to family members in their countries of origin, and about 10 percent of the aggregate $500 billion these workers earn each year is thought to go toward remittances. More than half of these remittance-senders are younger than thirty-five, and almost two-thirds are considered "working poor" or "lower middle class" by U.S. standards, with annual incomes of less than $30,000.

While some researchers worry that remittances lead to a cycle of dependency, most think that remittances can play a positive role in Latin American development. According to a prominent study of those in Latin America who receive remittances, 80 percent spend the funds on food, 48 percent on medication, 38 percent on education, 13 percent on mortgage payments, and 9 percent on savings.[36] Even expenditures on basic household goods can bolster local economies.[37] But more importantly, studies indicate that children from families receiving remittances are significantly more likely to remain in school, regardless of the educational level of the parents, a critical factor in development.[38]

---

[35] "Remittances 2007: A Bend in the Road or a New Direction?" Inter-American Development Bank, March 2008, available at http://idbdocs.iadb.org/wsdocs/getdocument.aspx?docnum=1381109.

[36] Orozco et al. "Transnational Engagement, Remittances and their Relationship to Development in Latin America and the Caribbean: Final Report," Institute for the Study of International Migration at Georgetown University, July 2005, available at http://isim.georgetown.edu/Publications/LindsayPubs/Rockefeller%20Report.pdf.

[37] David Seddon, "South Asian remittances: implications for development," *Contemporary South Asia*, Vol. 13, No. 4, December 2004, available at http://www.ingentaconnect.com/content/routledg/ccsa/2004/00000013/00000004/art00005.

[38] Ernesto Lopez-Cordova, "Improving health and education," *ID 21 Insights,* Vol. 60, January 2006, available at http://www.id21.org/insights/insights60/art02.html.

Some remittances are also channeled into productive investments, such as start-up capital for small businesses, a particularly positive use of funds.[39] A 2001 study showed that almost one-fifth of the capital invested in microenterprises in rural Mexico came from U.S. remittances.[40] A recent study by Bendixen and Associates states that in Mexico today, nearly 40 percent of remittance funds is going toward investment (the figure is 32 percent for Colombia and 25 percent for Guatemala).[41] These expenditures should have significant macro-level effects over time.

Another potentially positive factor for development is nonpermanent migration. Advances in communications and travel enable more "circular migration," in which people migrate for shorter periods of time or move back and forth repeatedly. In Latin America, such continuous migration has become an increasingly common strategy in the past six decades to increase and diversify family income. In the long term, it also means that migrants return to their home countries with new financial and human capital. For example, returning migrants are, according to recent research, more likely to engage in entrepreneurial activity. Mexicans who return from a seasonal agricultural workers program in Canada have been documented to invest in land and small businesses at home.[42] There is also evidence that Salvadorans and Dominicans start microenterprises upon returning from the United States.[43] Circulatory migration could have a particularly positive impact if extended to highly educated migrants. Although some have argued that Latin America is harmed by the emigration of highly skilled workers, recent research on China and India demonstrates that countries can

[39] Ibid. and Richard H. Adams Jr., "Remittances, Poverty, and Investment in Guatemala," in *International Migration, Remittances, and the Brain Drain*, edited by Çaglar Özden and Maurice Schiff (Washington, DC: World Bank; New York: Palgrave Macmillan, 2006).

[40] Christopher Woodruff and Rene Zenteno, "Remittances and Microenterprises in Mexico," Working Paper, Center for U.S.-Mexican Studies, University of California, San Diego, 2001.

[41] Presentation to World Bank Representatives, Bendixen and Associates, January 14, 2008.

[42] Tanya Basok, "Mexican Seasonal Migration to Canada and Development: A Community based Comparison," *International Migration,* Vol. 41, No. 2, 2003.

[43] José Itzigsohn, Carlos Dore Cabral, and Esther Hernandez Medina, "Mapping Dominican Transnationalism: Narrow and Broad Transnational Practices," *Ethnic and Racial Studies,* Vol. 22, No. 2, 1999, and Patricia Landolt, "Salvadoran Economic Transnationalism: Embedded Strategies for Household Maintenance, Immigrant Incorporation, and Entrepreneurial Expansion," *Global Networks: A Journal of Transnational Affairs,* Vol. 1, No. 3, 2001.

actually benefit from the migration of highly skilled professionals—producing "brain circulation," by which returning migrants bring human capital and technology with them, rather than causing "brain drain."[44] Technological advances suggest new potential for Latin American countries if they can secure the return of increasingly skilled migrants. However, restrictive immigration laws that bar immigrants from traveling freely back and forth and changing labor markets that provide more permanent year-round employment may be diminishing the potential benefits of migration.

The Task Force finds that migration and remittances benefit Latin American households by increasing disposable income and investment, but could prove risky in the long run if those with skills emigrate permanently. Domestic and international policies that promote circular migration and productive investment of remittances can maximize the positive impact of migration for sending countries.

Latin American Policy Responses to Migration

Latin American nations understand that the flow of goods and people are inextricably linked. As a result, efforts at economic integration have been matched with efforts at managing and facilitating immigration, with new domestic laws and new bilateral and multilateral migration accords. The Andean Community of Nations, for example, sees the unhampered movement of people as essential to forming an Andean Common Market. The participating countries have worked on such measures as developing complementary social-security arrangements among the participating countries, so that workers can be credited for payments made anywhere in the Andean Community. The Mercosur countries (Brazil, Argentina, Uruguay, and Paraguay) have also signed a Multilateral Agreement on Social Security to guarantee rights to all Mercosur residents in the subregion. A Mercosur Visa was approved in 2003, though it has yet to be implemented.

Argentina, the South American country that receives the greatest number of immigrants, has undertaken additional initiatives on its

---

[44] David Zweig et al., "Globalization and Transnational Human Capital: Overseas and Returnee Scholars to China," *China Quarterly*, Vol. 179, 2004.

own to address immigration flows. In 2003, it incorporated Mercosur legislation prohibiting discrimination based on national origin and guaranteeing increased access to health care and education. It has also signed bilateral migration agreements and memoranda of understanding with Bolivia and Peru to facilitate circular migration. Mexico, meanwhile, has adjusted its policies for the hundreds of thousands of U.S. retirees who have migrated south in recent years. For example, it now provides visas specifically for foreign retirees that give access to Mexico's health care system for a $300 annual premium. It also changed its laws to allow foreigners to own land outright rather than in trust, as previously required.

At the same time, in the absence of bilateral and multilateral agreements that apply to U.S.-bound migration, Latin American governments have begun developing their own policies, particularly focused on ways to encourage circular migration and remittance flows. While only four Latin American countries recognized dual citizenship in 1990, at least eleven countries do now. Colombian expatriates are allowed to elect representatives to the Colombian legislature; Dominicans can run for office in the Dominican Republic even when their primary residence is abroad; and Peruvians and Mexicans can now vote in elections in their countries of origin from abroad. Many governments have also started programs to encourage migrants to invest in their home countries and eventually return. Colombia and Uruguay have established incentives for returnee scholars and scientists. The Mexican government established the Program for Mexican Communities Living Abroad, which offers health, education, and legal advice to migrants and hometown organizations and encourages remittances for development projects. Some Mexican states have also established matching funds so that remittances intended for development projects are matched by states and cities. The Salvadoran government now has a Vice Ministry of Foreign Affairs for Salvadorans Abroad, whose vice minister helps migrants abroad and facilitates their return.

The Task Force finds that Latin American governments are pushing forward concrete policies to address the accelerating movement of people within the region as well as capitalize on migration to the United States. These efforts by Latin American governments help maintain ties between migrants and their countries of origin, and certain policies encourage migrants to remit and eventually return to their countries of origin. U.S. policies lag far behind those of Latin American governments in adapting to the realities of increased human mobility.

U.S. Immigration Policy

In 2006, the U.S. government authorized approximately 1.3 million immigrant visas, including approximately 800,000 for family-sponsored immigrants and 160,000 for employment-based immigrants. About 300,000 others received visas for other reasons, such as refugee and asylee status. That year, just over 800,000 people adjusted their migrant status and became legal permanent residents. As is often noted, the United States has always been a nation of immigrants. Immigration laws, however, have varied dramatically over time, from the fairly open policies of the nineteenth and early twentieth centuries to, starting in the 1920s, more restrictive policies based on national quotas and aimed at limiting immigration, especially from Asia and eastern and southern Europe. Since 1952, four principles have guided U.S. policy: the reunification of families; the admission of immigrants with needed skills; the protection of refugees; and the diversity of admissions by country of origin.

Immigration policy in the United States today is characterized by stringent laws and weak enforcement. In 1986, the Immigration Reform and Control Act (IRCA) provided amnesty to illegal immigrants who had entered the country before January 1, 1982, and criminalized the hiring of illegal workers, for the first time putting the onus on employers. But the law was not enforced and did not deter employers from hiring illegal immigrants. After the terrorist attacks of September 11, 2001, the federal government restructured the immigration bureaucracy, replacing the Immigration and Naturalization Service, which was part of the Justice Department, with Immigration and Customs Enforcement, a branch of the newly formed Department of Homeland Security. This change, which combined an antiterrorism mandate with responsibility to control U.S.-bound migration, resulted in increased resources for border patrols and surveillance equipment. All together, current policies create substantial impediments for legal migration. As a result, they encourage Latin Americans (and others) to enter the United States illegally. And once they are in the United States, immigrants are more likely to stay, since getting into the country is expensive and risky. There are roughly twelve million illegal immigrants in the United States today.

The overhaul of immigration policy proposed in 2007 would have provided a means for legalization of these immigrants. It also would have eliminated the system that prioritized family unification for one based on points that reflected skills, English proficiency, family ties, and U.S. economic needs. It would have established a larger guest worker program as well as increased border security. Employers would have been held responsible for verifying workers' legal status. But despite a major push by the Bush administration and support from major figures in both parties, the proposal did not withstand political furor or questions over how effective it would have been in controlling immigration or disciplining employers. With the failure of reform legislation in Congress in 2007, and the fact that no new attempt at comprehensive reform is likely until after the 2008 presidential election, state and local governments have increasingly been creating their own policies to handle immigrants—in some cases going out of their way to welcome immigrants, in others seeking to be more restrictive. Despite the fact that some of these policies have been found unconstitutional, this trend is likely to continue.

The failures of U.S. immigration policy affect national security, economic growth, and foreign relations. The status quo fails even to meet the most basic objective of guaranteeing proper documentation of visitors and noncitizen residents. It concentrates almost solely on the U.S.-Mexico border, despite the fact that nearly half of unauthorized workers in the United States enter legally through other ports and overstay their visas. It also fails to address the fact that, with historically low unemployment rates and an aging population, the United States will need more workers to fill (and keep) jobs within the domestic economy. This labor shortage will only become more acute in the coming decades, as baby boomers retire. To maintain GDP growth, a sizable number of migrant workers will be needed across all skill levels.

Finally, the failures of U.S. immigration policy have become a foreign policy problem. In the United States, immigration is largely considered a domestic policy issue. But given the profound impact that U.S. immigration policy has on many Latin American nations, it is naturally considered a vital issue in their relations with the United States. The tenor of recent immigration debates and the failure to pass meaningful immigration reform have hurt U.S. standing in the region, as many Latin American nations (including those without large populations in the United States) perceive current laws as discriminatory and unfair toward their citizens.

The Task Force finds that comprehensive immigration reform is necessary to create a system that better meets U.S. security, economic, and foreign policy interests, and must be a priority for the next administration. A system that offers incentives to migrate legally, to work hard and gain skills while in the United States, and to return to the countries of origin eventually with the acquired capital and skills would not only benefit the United States, it would also foster economic and political development in Latin America.

Energy

U.S. anxieties over dependence on foreign energy resources are usually centered on the Middle East, but the United States relies on the western hemisphere (including Canada) for nearly half its oil.[45] Recently, resurgent resource nationalism, production bottlenecks, and the politicization of energy trade have raised concerns that Latin America may become a less reliable supplier and drive up global energy prices. At the same time, the region presents abundant opportunities for new investment in traditional and alternative energy resources—making it critical that U.S. and Latin American governments both confront the energy challenge and seize the opportunity of greater cooperation.

Traditional Energy Supplies: Stalling Production and Integration

Latin America provides nearly 30 percent of the United States' foreign oil. Mexico—which, via its state oil company Petróleos Mexicanos (PEMEX), has about 1 percent of known world oil reserves and produces some 3 million barrels a day—is the United States' third most important petroleum source, following Canada and Saudi Arabia. It currently accounts for 11 percent of U.S. oil imports. However, rising domestic demand, declining productivity, and depleted reserves threaten the country's position as an energy-exporting nation. The Cantarell

---

[45] "U.S. Imports by Country of Origin," Energy Information Administration, available at http://tonto.eia.doe.gov/dnav/pet/pet_move_impcus_a2_nus_ep00_im0_mbbl_m.htm.

oil field is facing sharp declines in production, and new exploration is hampered by inadequate investment. Over 60 percent of PEMEX's revenues go to the government's budget, and private and/or foreign investment in the oil sector remains largely prohibited (in accordance with the Mexican Constitution), leaving only limited opportunities for foreign participation. In the short term, it remains unlikely that the divided Mexican Congress will approve private sector investment,[46] and even if the reformist Calderón government is able to loosen current investment restrictions, new production would take years to come online. Without significant changes, some analysts predict, Mexico may become a net importer of oil in as few as ten years. For the United States, this development would impel a dramatic and difficult shift in energy sourcing.

There are some positive trends in the U.S.-Mexico energy relationship as well, however. Energy integration in North America has proceeded. Extensive cross-border networks of modern pipelines and power lines, tariff-free trade across borders, technology sharing, and constant contact between energy officials in both countries have facilitated fluid commerce and constant dialogue. The North America Energy Working Group (NAEWG), an organization of midlevel career energy officials from Mexico, the United States, and Canada established in 2001, has sponsored several valuable regional energy studies, compiled standardized energy statistics, and begun to reach out to various public and private stakeholders in relevant industries.

Venezuela, the ninth-largest producer of oil in the world, the fourth-largest supplier to the United States, and the location of 6.6 percent of the world's proven reserves, also faces challenges. Since 2001, President Chávez has sought to use his nation's vast energy wealth for public programs and for his own ambitions by strengthening government control over the state-owned oil company Petróleos de Venezuela (PDVSA), limiting foreign ownership of joint ventures, and demanding higher royalty payments from foreign oil companies. Riding a wave of high prices, Venezuela has devoted much of its oil revenues to funding government programs and foreign policy initiatives—by

---

[46] David Shields, "Pemex en el Contexto de su Crisis de Reservas y Producción," *Foreign Affairs en Español*, July-September 2007.

directly subsidizing supplies to sympathetic nations, especially in Central America and the Caribbean—rather than robust reinvestment. While these choices may boost Chávez's domestic popularity and win him regional allies, they have diminished PDVSA's efficiency and led to production declines. In response to the Chávez government's demands for a majority stake in all joint oil ventures, a number of private multinationals have curtailed further investment in the exploitation of difficult-to-access, but potentially lucrative, crude reserves, while others have decided to close operations altogether. Joint ventures with state-owned companies from China, Iran, Brazil, and other nations may help to fill this void, but flat midterm production prospects coupled with rising internal demand are likely to limit export increases (and perhaps lead to declines) in the coming years.

Given the importance of Venezuela as a supplier, any decline in exports would have problematic implications for the United States. President Chávez has also repeatedly threatened to divert significant portions of Venezuela's U.S.-bound oil to China. However, existing symmetries and low transportation costs between Venezuelan heavy crude production and U.S.-based refineries make such a dramatic shift unlikely in the short run. In fact, even though Venezuelan production has fallen since 2001, oil exports to the United States have remained relatively stable (with the exception of a two-month strike in 2002–2003 during which the oil sector virtually shut down).[47]

Ecuador and Brazil are or could be other important sources of oil for the region and for the United States. In Ecuador, political turmoil and resurgent resource nationalism have created an uncertain investment environment. Relations with Washington have been particularly tense since the government took over the operations of Occidental Petroleum and Rafael Correa was elected in 2006. Brazil has stepped up exploration, thanks in large part to the expertise of state-controlled Petróleo Brasileiro (Petrobras) and friendly terms offered to foreign investors. The recent Tupi oil find—estimated at five billion to eight billion barrels—could place Brazil ahead of Canada and Mexico in terms of reserves, second

---

[47] "Energy Security: Issues Related to Potential Reductions in Venezuelan Oil Production," United States Government Accountability Office, June 2006, available at http://www.gao.gov/new.items/d06668.pdf.

only to Venezuela in the hemisphere. Other as-yet-unmeasured discoveries may bolster Brazil's reserves even further. Largely energy self-sufficient already, an increase in Brazilian oil exports could substantially benefit not only Brazil but also the United States.

Latin America's natural gas resources also have the potential to play an important part in U.S. energy security in the coming years. The United States is currently able to meet most of its natural gas needs. But owing to the environmental advantages of natural gas and cost-saving improvements in liquefied natural gas (LNG) processing and transportation, demand will likely increase considerably—by 0.6 percent a year from 2004 to 2030, according to the Energy Information Administration's *International Energy Outlook 2007*—which U.S. and Canadian supplies will be unable to meet. With reserves equal to those of North America, South America's natural gas market will become an important foreign energy source.

Peru is already set to take advantage of these developments, with long-awaited LNG exports from the Camisea reserves in the south set to come online, and several commitments for Peru to export LNG to the U.S. West Coast and Mexico already in place. In other places, however—Bolivia, most notably—political turmoil is thwarting the potential of greater natural gas production and export. Potential Bolivian exports to Chile and the United States have been held up by anti-Chilean sentiment and resource nationalism. (The protests that followed a 2003 investment and export proposal helped bring down a president.) Bolivia's 2006 nationalization caused problems for importers, especially Brazil and Argentina, and the uncertain operating environment has brought new investment in the natural gas sector to a halt. Other regional energy integration proposals, such as the Gasoducto del Sur, an over 9,000-kilometer pipeline linking future Venezuelan natural gas fields to markets in Brazil, Argentina, Paraguay, Uruguay, and perhaps even Chile, have also been put on hold.[48]

---

[48] Another important proposed natural gas pipeline—the so-called South American gas ring (suggested in response to Bolivia's political turmoil since 2000)—would ship gas from Camisea in Peru around Bolivia to supply the Southern Cone market, potentially undercutting Bolivia's strategic position in the region. Apart from the political difficulties that such a plan would cause (the project might link Camisea in southern Peru to northern Chile, directly through the territory that Bolivia seeks for its corridor to the sea), it too is plagued by a number of logistical, financial, and technical difficulties.

The rise of resource nationalism represents a difficult challenge for both the United States and Latin American countries. One side effect of this has been the decline of high-level multilateral energy forums, further lessening the likelihood that political, financial, environmental, and other impediments will be tackled aggressively. In particular, the termination of the Western Hemisphere energy ministers meetings (held annually between 1999 and 2004 under U.S. leadership and the rubric of the Summit of the Americas process) has left a void. While South American leaders pledged at an April 2007 regional energy summit to initiate a ministerial-level South American Energy Council, the success of this effort is far from assured. Infrastructure deficiencies are another obstacle. According to the International Energy Agency (IEA), in order to meet increased energy demands, Latin America will require close to $1.3 trillion in overall investment in the energy sector between 2001 and 2030, the equivalent of 1.5 percent of GDP each year.[49] The sheer size of the deficiency should encourage Latin American governments to adjust regulatory frameworks and provide opportunities for public and private investment from the United States and around the world.

The Task Force finds that Latin America remains a relatively stable oil-producing region and potentially an important source of natural gas exports, though state ownership and political turmoil limit international and private sector involvement in some countries, impeding efficiency and growth. Future output will depend on substantial investments in exploration and production, favoring the energy sectors in countries more open to investment, expanded collaboration, and trade. In these nations, in particular Brazil, Mexico, and Peru, the extent of dialogue and collaboration taking place among Mexico, Canada, and the United States should serve as a positive model. Expanding and stabilizing the energy trade across the region would have important benefits to economic development, political stability, and the U.S.-Latin America relationship.

---

[49] Veronica Prado, "Energy Infrastructure in the Western Hemisphere," *Energy Cooperation in the Western Hemisphere: Benefits and Impediments,* edited by Sidney Weintraub et al. (Washington, DC: Center for Strategic and International Studies, 2007), p. 406.

New Directions: Promoting Alternative Energy Sources

As the United States and other nations look to diversify their energy sources and reduce dependence on oil, Latin America presents a unique opportunity for engagement and cooperation. Latin America already leads the United States in the production and use of hydroelectric power, which supplies 23 percent of its energy needs (as compared to less than 3 percent in the United States).[50] The region has also made investments in solar- and wind-powered technologies, particularly in Argentina, Brazil, and Chile. Cooperation on alternative energy research and production could become an important component of U.S.-Latin America relations in the years ahead. Partnering with Latin American nations in the development of alternative energy sources would allow the United States to build and deepen diplomatic relationships through joint initiatives on development, climate change, and environmental sustainability. Two areas in particular—biofuels and nuclear energy—present important and immediate opportunities.

Only in the past several years have scarcity in oil markets, environmental awareness, scientific advances, and proactive subsidy policies combined to make biofuels, notably ethanol and biodiesel, reasonably price competitive with petroleum products on a wider scale. Biofuels now provide an opportunity for Latin America and the United States to assume global leadership in a sector of future competitive and environmental value (namely, decreased greenhouse gas emissions).

Brazil and the United States are currently the largest producers of ethanol in the world (with 38 and 50 percent of global production in 2007, respectively).[51] Brazil has become a global leader in the promotion of sugar-based ethanol usage through the implementation of flex-fuel technology, mandatory fuel blends, and infrastructure investment. In 2006, domestic consumption of ethanol accounted for nearly half of Brazilian passenger vehicle fuel supply by volume (in the United States,

---

[50] "Statistical Review of World Energy," British Petroleum, 2007, available at http://www.bp.com/productlanding.do?categoryId = 6848&contentId = 7033471.

[51] "Industry Statistics," Renewable Fuels Association, available at http://www.ethanolrfa.org/industry/statistics.

the figure was 4 percent). Today, close to 90 percent of all new automobiles produced in Brazil use flex-fuel technology.

Other nations following Brazil's lead are considering their own potential in this area: Guatemala, Costa Rica, and El Salvador have the right climate and well-developed sugar industries, while Honduras and Colombia are looking forward to producing biodiesel based on palm. After a series of high-profile meetings between Presidents Bush and Lula da Silva, the United States and Brazil launched a Biofuels Partnership in April 2007, pledging to expand technical assistance to nations in Central America and the Caribbean with the goal of commoditizing ethanol, first regionally and then globally.

Protectionism remains a significant challenge to building a global biofuels market; however, the negative consequences of external oil dependence have led some to concentrate on greater energy self-sufficiency through the development of domestic biofuel industries, and by introducing subsidies, tax breaks, and tariffs. In the United States, efforts have concentrated on corn-based ethanol, which is widely recognized to be less cost- and energy-efficient than sugar-based production techniques.[52] Nonetheless, the corn industry enjoys substantial government support, as well as significant tariff protection from its Brazilian competitors.[53] These policies may hinder the development of freer biofuel commodity markets, discouraging longer-term investments.

Latin America has also seen resurgent interest in nuclear power. A little over forty years ago, there appeared to be a genuine risk of a nuclear arms race in the region—a trend that was short-circuited by the establishment of a Nuclear Weapons Free Zone by the 1967 Treaty of Tlatelolco. Since then, Argentina, Brazil, and Mexico have built seven nuclear power plants, although only Argentina has established a strong technical capacity in this area—a capacity that recently has been

---

[52] 0.74 BTUs of fossil fuel are required to produce 1 BTU of corn-based ethanol, while only 0.12 BTUs of fossil fuel are required to produce 1 BTU of sugar-based ethanol. Corn-based ethanol costs approximately $1.14 per gallon, while sugar-based ethanol costs $0.83 per gallon.

[53] Some Brazilian ethanol still enters the United States directly or via Caribbean countries, where it goes through a final refining process and then can enter the U.S. market duty-free under DR-CAFTA or the Caribbean Basin Initiative, up to an established quota.

tapped by Venezuela to explore the possible development of a nuclear energy program of its own. Today there is a compelling argument for the expansion of nuclear energy, which provides base power with zero greenhouse gas emissions, as Brazil's construction of new reactors and use of nuclear-powered submarines attest. However, achieving such expansion will require that Latin America address the complex challenges of managing and disposing of uranium and nuclear waste and meeting international standards (especially given concerns over Chávez's desire for nuclear-enrichment capability and a relationship with Iran).

The Task Force finds that although biofuels will not displace oil and gas, they can help diversify energy choices, lower the energy intensity of national economies, decrease greenhouse gas emissions, and foster greater energy security for the entire hemisphere. While being mindful of the need to guarantee food security, diversifying energy sources could be an important driver of economic development in Latin America as the region becomes an important technology, production, and research hub in the long-term development of a global biofuels market. Expanding nuclear power would further efforts at energy diversification. Cooperation on such issues provides a unique opportunity for the United States to reengage Latin America proactively, with shared environmental and energy concerns deepening diplomatic relationships.[54]

---

[54] Most biofuel production in Latin America today is labor intensive. Expanded biofuel industries are thus likely to create jobs in agriculture and transport. However, some activists worry that most of the jobs are low-wage agricultural in nature, ensuring substandard conditions. Increased mechanization, as in the U.S. industry, is likely to limit labor demand.

Recommendations

Geographic proximity, economic, social, and cultural integration, and shared democratic values inextricably link the United States and Latin America, influencing U.S. society and directly affecting U.S. national interests. The next administration and Congress will have a critical opportunity to reframe and redirect U.S. relations with the region. This report is intended to steer policy toward the four crucial areas outlined in this report: poverty and inequality, public security, migration, and energy security. In doing so, the United States will better promote its traditional goals of economic expansion, democratic consolidation, and narcotics control in the region.

In rethinking its policies, the United States must recognize its own limitations. U.S. resources and policy tools cannot refashion the domestic policies and economies of Latin America. But by better targeting its resources, the United States can aid Latin America's own efforts while advancing U.S. interests in the security and prosperity of the entire region.

The Task Force underscores the importance of Latin America to the United States regardless of high-priority foreign policy issues elsewhere, and urges the next U.S. president to commit to work cooperatively with all Latin American countries—and Canada—to respond to shared challenges. *To do so, the Task Force recommends that U.S. policy toward the region should complement Latin America-led initiatives to alleviate poverty and enhance public security.* Comprehensive U.S. immigration law reform is vital, and mutual cooperation toward alternative energy is a win–win proposition.

Lessening Poverty and Structural Inequality

Reducing poverty and improving access to market opportunities in Latin America are central to U.S. objectives of promoting stable democratic government, enabling economic expansion, and providing alternatives to illegal economic activity. It is in the U.S. interest to support those Latin American governments that are seeking to decrease poverty and structural inequality.

Support Local and Regional Solutions

The Task Force urges the next administration to convene a public/private summit on poverty and inequality during its first year in office in order to review "best practices" in the region and to demonstrate U.S. commitment to work with Latin American governments and other stakeholders in addressing these problems. This forum would bring together government officials, private businesses, multilateral institutions, and NGOs from Latin American countries, the United States, and other involved nations, including the European Union and China.

Increase Public Revenues

Latin American governments must establish the institutional infrastructure necessary to boost public revenues if they are to confront social and economic problems successfully. In addition to encouraging increased tax collection through new administrative and enforcement measures, the United States should encourage countries to institute more progressive tax systems, moving away from relying primarily on regressive and cyclical VATs and import duties, to a more progressive mix of property, personal, corporate, capital gains, and other taxes. EU aid practices have begun to reflect such concerns. *The Task Force recommends that U.S. officials encourage the International Monetary Fund and other international and multilateral financial institutions to incorporate the redistributive nature of tax systems and revenue collection in their reviews of fiscal policy and their arrangements with borrowing nations. The Task Force also supports increasing U.S. aid and expertise to assist in restructuring tax systems and building the infrastructure and judicial capacity necessary to increase tax collection and limit tax evasion.*

The United States should also encourage the formalization of informal enterprises. While primarily a domestic issue for Latin American governments, the United States should offer, through multilateral institutions such as the World Bank and Inter-American Development Bank, technical assistance to help reform regulatory structures, streamline business registration and incorporation requirements, integrate labor, and improve credit and property registries. This formalization will benefit workers and increase future tax revenues, providing governments greater capacity to address the needs of their citizens.

Promote More Open Trade

The $600 million in U.S. poverty-oriented aid to Latin America every year pales in comparison with the $555 billion in annual trade. Through trade, accordingly, the United States has an important opportunity to further economic development. While previous trade agreements have provided mutual benefits, the often uncompromising protection and/or subsidization of particular U.S. economic sectors has limited the economic growth and poverty-reducing effects of trade and, in some cases, heightened the dislocations associated with economic opening. The United States should promote more open trade in areas of Latin American comparative advantage as an important step to reduce poverty and inequality in the region, which will further broaden long-term economic opportunities for Latin America and the United States.

While recognizing the political challenges and the importance of multilateral solutions, the Task Force recommends that the next administration proactively support the liberalization of textile and agricultural policies, including reducing and eventually eliminating tariffs and subsidies on agricultural commodities, including tariffs on ethanol, and relaxing rules of origin requirements on textiles. Further U.S. opening in these areas would position the United States to seek the further opening of economic sectors in Latin America important to U.S. businesses, such as services. It would also lower overall costs for U.S. consumers.[55] To do this the United States should

---

[55] Arvind Panagariya, "Liberalizing Agriculture," *Foreign Affairs,* December 2005, and Jessica X. Fan et al., "Are apparel trade restrictions regressive?" *Journal of Consumer Affairs*, Vol. 32, No. 2, Winter 1998.

work with Brazil, other Latin American countries, and European nations to push forward the Doha Development Agenda.

At the same time, the United States cannot ignore the impetus of globalization. All countries benefit from programs that lessen the dislocations that result from technological change and market opening. The United States should host a hemispheric conference on globalization, trade, technology, and social support in order to explore the best ways to construct social safety nets appropriate for today's economy.

The United States should also approve pending free trade agreements with Colombia and Panama. Free trade remains an important policy tool for expanding economic opportunities in the region and the United States. Rejection of these agreements would severely damage close allies, send a negative signal to other countries in the region, give rise to the view that the United States is an unreliable partner, and strengthen countries in the region that espouse anti-Americanism. The United States should also extend trade preferences to Bolivia and Ecuador as a way to maintain useful relations with these complex countries. Abruptly ending these ties would serve quickly to push these countries further away from the United States diplomatically, and could destabilize already weak institutions in politically fractious countries.

Increase and Refocus Targeted Assistance

U.S. funding for targeted assistance and antipoverty programs should reflect the priorities of Latin American governments (as established in the first-year public/private summit on poverty) and also involve restructuring and integrating the programs of various U.S. government bureaucracies to focus on crisis areas in the region.

The Task Force recommends that the next U.S. administration and Congress continue and expand their targeted assistance in the following ways:

• Fully fund the Millennium Challenge Account.

• Complement these programs with new initiatives that reach the poor regions of large middle-income countries—such as Brazil and Mexico—that are currently ineligible for MCA assistance. Within these and the MCA programs, target both poverty alleviation and institution-building.

- Change the implementation rules of aid programs in Congress to allow NGOs and contractors from the recipient countries, with appropriate supervision and accountability, to design and implement aid programs, providing more domestic jobs and opportunities.
- Direct more counternarcotics aid toward developing alternative economic opportunities to narcotics production.
- Use U.S. influence in multilateral institutions, particularly the World Bank, the Inter-American Development Bank, and the Overseas Private Investment Corporation, to promote financial inclusion by expanding microenterprise and small-business financing. This should include financial literacy programs, as well as technical assistance regarding the regulatory frameworks and information systems necessary for private banks to enter these markets.

Enhancing Security in the Hemisphere

The United States can support Latin American efforts to meet security threats by offering resources and expertise aimed at improving law enforcement, judicial institutions, and public transparency and accountability.

Build Capacity and Strengthen Cooperation

Improving public security requires strengthening the rule of law throughout Latin America. In the end, these changes must come from Latin American governments themselves. Nevertheless, the United States can play a positive role by offering support for security sector and judicial reform, regional cooperation, and information sharing.

The Task Force recommends that U.S. assistance focus on law enforcement and judicial reform in Latin America. While the United States is already involved in some of these programs, they should be expanded both in breadth and depth, to assist in, among other things, police training. The United States should also offer expanded investigative and prosecutorial training and expertise in judicial transparency, in order to encourage the professionalization of judicial institutions.

The United States should also encourage greater international cooperation at national, state, and local levels by expanding information exchanges. These include building on pilot programs, such as the one between Rio de Janeiro and Boston city police, that promote department-level interactions between U.S. and Latin American forces. It also includes exchanges between Latin American governments, law enforcement agencies, and civil society organizations to evaluate programs and practices in other countries and regions and promote innovative solutions to security problems.

Address Both Supply and Demand in Counternarcotics

Illegal narcotics represent a complex social, institutional, and legal challenge worldwide, and are a paramount concern of U.S. policymakers. The United States should establish a comprehensive drug policy that addresses both supply and demand. To combat supply, the United States should continue to work closely with Latin American governments and regional organizations on eradication and interdiction and, in line with these recommendations, on targeting U.S. aid to institution-building, anticorruption, and poverty-alleviation efforts. The United States should continue to assist Colombia in its counternarcotics and counterinsurgent initiatives with aid packages similar to the one approved by Congress in 2007, which established a better balance between military and police aid and economic and social assistance, especially with respect to the rule of law. Continued emphasis in Plan Colombia on prosecuting human rights violations and political violence, including offenses committed by former and reconstituted paramilitary members, whether against labor leaders or any other member of Colombian civil society, will remain critical to creating a stable environment.

As with all crime, professionalization of law enforcement and judicial institutions is crucial. Only by rooting out corruption and ensuring that criminals face justice will the cycle of impunity end. Given the importance of Latin American militaries in counternarcotics strategies, current U.S. assistance should continue. In the long run, however, civilian police forces that operate independently to combat the drug trade and crime are critically important for consolidating democratic institutions. Over time, the security functions in these countries should shift significantly to law enforcement institutions. To aid this process, the United States should offer greater assistance to Latin American governments for training and equipping competent police forces to take on the obligations that in some countries currently involve the military.

The United States must recognize that a long-term solution to the narcotics problem will require reducing the demand for, together with the supply of, drugs. As long as a lucrative U.S. drug market (estimated at more than $60 billion) exists, strong demand pull will continue to channel illegal drugs to the United States. The U.S. government should focus on domestic prevention, enforcement, and rehabilitation. In addition, as worldwide drug consumption grows, it is crucial for the United States to work with other nations in combating this transnational threat. The United States should push the European Union in particular to share the financial and logistical burden of counternarcotics strategies and to be more effective in addressing the broader demand side for illegal substances. This will require consultation, information sharing, and an expansion of U.S. policy priorities.

Control Guns and Money Flows

The millions of guns—and especially illegal guns—in the hands of Latin Americans erode state control and increase violence. Many of these weapons come from the United States. The United States should commit to control the flow of guns into Latin America better by:

- Supporting a binding international arms trade treaty that establishes international standards to regulate the international transfer of conventional arms, with real backing from the five permanent members of the UN Security Council and above all from the United States.

- Ratifying and ensuring compliance with the Inter-American Convention Against the Illicit Manufacturing of and Trafficking in Firearms, Ammunition, Explosives, and other Related Materials.

In addition to weapons, drug traffickers depend on the ability to "clean" illegal profits. The United States should strengthen current anti–money laundering initiatives by:

- Working closely with Latin American counterparts, and particularly with Mexican authorities, to continue regulating foreign exchange companies, or "casas de cambio," that process large amounts of drug money.

- Improving monitoring of border flows from the United States to Mexico, since bulk cash smuggling is the principal method for moving drug money out of the United States. This should be done in conjunction with illegal arms trafficking initiatives.

- Creating a system similar to the CIA-based Foreign Terrorist Asset Tracking Group for the dissemination of intelligence, diplomatic, regulatory, and law enforcement information related to narcotics-based money laundering. All information relating to narcotics financing should be centrally analyzed and distributed to all relevant policy-makers.

- Ensuring that the Financial Crimes Enforcement Network (FinCEN), the bureau of the Treasury Department that combats money laundering and financial crimes, has adequate resources to target narcotics-related money laundering.

Collaborate to Dismantle Transnational Gangs

Gangs operate cross border in many Central American countries and the United States. The United States should work to impede the expansion of these transnational gangs by:

- Increasing information sharing with Central American and Caribbean investigative and police institutions, including disclosure of the full criminal records of U.S. deportees (not just the crime that led to deportation), so that proper measures can be taken by the receiving countries.

- Increasing the $50 million set aside in the Merida Initiative for Central American nations. These funds should be used for police professionalization, which will aid in the fight against drug trafficking as well as transnational gangs.

Reforming Immigration Policy

Immigration reform is one of the most pressing domestic policy issues facing the United States. It is also a critical issue for U.S.-Latin America relations. The defeat of immigration reform in the U.S. Senate in 2007 suggests that no broad national policy change will be forthcoming in the near term. Piecemeal measures implemented by states and cities are no substitute for a coherent federal policy on immigration. The next president and Congress must face this issue in order to meet U.S. security, economic, and foreign policy interests better.

The Task Force urges the next administration and Congress to negotiate and approve comprehensive immigration reform in 2009. Viable immigration policy must: improve border security and management; address the unauthorized work force already here; ensure employer security, verification, and responsibility; and expand a flexible worker program to meet changing U.S. economic demands.

Initiatives to improve border security must address the flow of goods and people across all U.S. borders and ports of entry. *Notwithstanding this broader requirement, the Task Force recommends closer cooperation with Mexican law enforcement authorities, particularly for the interdiction of illegal crime and human smuggling networks that operate along our shared border.* Passage of the Merida Initiative would be an initial step toward helping to strengthen Mexican law enforcement capacity and deepening formal ties and cooperation between the two countries' security forces.

Immigration reform must include regularizing the status of the estimated twelve million unauthorized workers currently in the United States. Deportation or "attrition through enforcement" are not realistic options to meet U.S. goals of improving security and lessening the consequences for the U.S. work force. Instead, Congress should permit a form of earned adjustment that authorizes these twelve million individuals and their activities within the United States.[56]

The Task Force believes that the United States should reformulate its immigration policy to encourage circular migration. This would allow immigrants to come to the United States for a set period of time, improve their own economic situation while also contributing to the U.S. economy, and then return home with new human and financial capital, creating the potential for longer-term economic development in their home communities and countries. To be successful, policy reforms should:

---

[56] The Council on Foreign Relations is currently sponsoring an Independent Task Force report on immigration policy that is scheduled to be released in 2009.

- Provide longer and more flexible labor contracts. To promote circularity, contracts must be long enough to allow migrants to recover financial costs associated with migration and save enough money to establish businesses upon return. Restrictive policies, such as those limiting workers to stays of a few years, could be self-defeating, as workers generally have strong incentives to overstay their visas.

- Provide options for reentry so that migrants participating in seasonal work can travel between countries during the working season, reinforcing ties and the likelihood of return.

- Encourage remittances through programs in the formal banking system to extend financial services to immigrants. This will enable less costly means of transferring money and saving for productive investment in their home communities.

- Target migrants returning to their home countries through existing USAID and multilateral-institution technical assistance and capacity-building programs, supporting these individuals' efforts to reestablish their community ties and invest in local business ventures.

Coordinate with Sending Countries to Regulate Migratory Flows

Given the high percentage of immigrants from particular Latin American countries, the United States should pursue bilateral or multilateral immigration agreements with these nations. Ongoing cooperation on migration should be a mainstay of the bilateral agenda between the United States and the main origin countries. Bilateral or multilateral agreements, such as those already being developed among Latin American nations, can ensure that the rights of migrants are respected, that they are working in sectors in need of labor, and that they are not posing a security threat to the receiving country. Through these agreements, the United States could certify labor shortages in particular sectors of the economy. The countries could, in turn, enact measures that ensure that temporary workers do in fact return home after their stays. These formal agreements should include provisions to make earned health and pension benefits portable, as well as provide information to expatriated workers on projects, jobs, and other opportunities within their home countries to encourage return.

Developing and Diversifying Energy Sources

There is a unique opportunity in the energy sector for genuine and constructive collaboration and cooperation between Latin American nations and the United States by addressing the growing challenges of energy security and climate change.

Promote Cooperation and Investment in Traditional Energy Sources

In the oil and gas sectors, more effective production and extraction will increase worldwide energy supply and put downward pressure on prices. While U.S. influence is limited (particularly with the growing role of national oil companies in the region and worldwide), it can encourage two developments. *First, the Task Force recommends supporting the creation of subregional and regional energy working groups on the model of the North American Energy Working Group.* To depoliticize energy cooperation, such organizations should concentrate on technical issues such as data exchange, electricity connectivity, fuel standards, infrastructure protection, environmental sustainability, and lessons learned. *Second, the Task Force recommends that the United States actively support environmentally sustainable energy infrastructure financing in Latin America through multilateral lending institutions and foreign direct investment.* In particular, the United States can facilitate funding for the last stages of Peru's Camisea natural gas project.

Develop Alternative Energy Markets

The Western Hemisphere produces 80 percent of the world's biofuels, and a precedent for collaborative leadership has been established by the U.S.-Brazil initiative, which includes cooperation on standards to facilitate trade, technology distribution, and support for the development of biofuel production in other countries. The expansion of these industries, aided by U.S. domestic and foreign policy incentives, can benefit the environment, foster economic development through technology transfer and adaptation, and aid in poverty reduction through job creation in the hemisphere. *The Task Force recommends building on the U.S.-Brazil Biofuels Pact to encourage the development of alternative energy in the region.* The most important policy steps are domestic, including removing disincentives for hemisphere production and trade in biofuels and creating incentives for U.S. gas distributors to increase the availability of biofuels.

The Task Force also recommends that the United States encourage the production of alternative fuels and their use by creating a Western Hemisphere umbrella initiative for sustained collaboration and long-term cooperation with regional partners. This would include:

- Creating a Hemispheric Alternative Energy Initiative to develop capacity and infrastructure, encourage innovation, and address issues related to biofuels such as food security and environmental protection.

- Establishing a formal working group with Brazil, Argentina, and Mexico to discuss issues associated with the expansion of nuclear energy, in accordance with the International Atomic Energy Agency rules, and to collaborate on efforts that are both economically and environmentally sustainable.

- Promoting the production of alternative energies, such as wind and solar, through new incentives and trade missions sponsored by the secretary of commerce, and World Bank, IDB, and International Finance Corporation financing.

Broadening Diplomacy

While the United States maintains productive relationships with the vast majority of Latin American nations, there are a few with which the United States has strained relations. *The Task Force finds that the United States must officially recognize all countries in the region and should work to identify areas of common interest and cooperation in order to advance U.S. interests, regardless of the countries' political identity; this includes Cuba and Venezuela.*

The United States should continue to voice strong support for democracy and to express concern when it perceives that governments are failing to maintain democratic institutions and basic human rights practices. But it should not cut diplomatic ties in such cases. By ignoring and isolating certain nations in our hemisphere, the United States reduces its own influence in these countries and precludes dialogue through which mutual interests can be addressed; at the same time, it inadvertently strengthens the regimes in these countries, as the experience with Cuba amply demonstrates. U.S. relations with Brazil and Mexico should also be strengthened and expanded.

Deepen U.S. Relations with Brazil

Brazil is the fourth-largest democracy and the ninth-largest economy in the world, and it has become an increasingly important actor not only in Latin America but globally. *The Task Force recommends that the United States build on its existing and welcome collaboration with Brazil on ethanol to develop a more consistent, coordinated, and broader partnership that incorporates a wide range of bilateral, regional, and global issues.* One crucial area for partnership is regional security. Expanding on current peacekeeping efforts, the United States should broaden and deepen regional security cooperation with Brazil. The narcotics trade threatens Brazil's security, as it is an important transit country for the European drug market and increasingly a consumer country of cocaine and other drugs. Increasing Brazilian involvement in the fight against narcotics through government-to-government cooperation and joint security initiatives will not only ease the U.S. burden in the war on drugs, but will also make U.S. and Brazilian efforts more effective.

The United States should also work closely with Brazil to push forward the Doha Round of global trade negotiations. While this would mean changing domestic agricultural policies, U.S. negotiators could then aggressively pursue more open markets in U.S. areas of concern.

Finally, energy and climate change provide ample opportunity for deepening ties and securing mutual economic and environmental advantages. Both the United States and Brazil are increasingly turning to LNG to satisfy future energy demands. The United States should work together with Brazil to develop the LNG hemispheric market, benefiting both countries' energy matrixes. On biofuels, the United States should pursue a broader joint policy initiative that promotes the development of environmentally sensitive alternative fuels in the region and around the world.

Strengthen Cooperation with Mexico

Few countries are as important for U.S. safety and security as Mexico. Mexico is the United States' third-largest trading partner (after Canada and China), with $330 billion worth of goods crossing the border each year. It is the third-largest supplier of oil to the United States. Nearly two-thirds of the forty-five million Latinos in the United States are Mexican descendants, and Mexico is currently the largest supplier of new immigrants, legal and illegal. Even as NAFTA has driven economic integration, official U.S.-Mexico relations lag behind what is a de facto social and economic integration between these two countries. The United States has a vital interest in the stability and prosperity of Mexico, which, in large measure, depends on the continued consolidation of Mexico's democratic institutions and on closing the gap in the standards of living between Mexico and the United States.

Security cooperation is becoming increasingly central to U.S.-Mexico relations. The recently announced Merida Initiative would, if passed by Congress, provide $1.4 billion worth of equipment and training in the next three years to assist Mexico in its fight against escalating drug violence. This proposal recognizes Mexico as an important partner in facing the mutual challenge of narcotics trafficking. *The Task Force supports this program, but calls for an extension in funding for police and judicial reform and training. In particular, it should emphasize the professionalization of state and local (as opposed to national) police forces.*

Energy remains an important area of mutual interest. The United States should focus on the prospects for boosting oil and gas production by promoting U.S. company service contracts (allowed under existing Mexican law) and through assistance in the ultra-deep waters of the Gulf of Mexico. The United States should also stand ready to spur investment in PEMEX when and if the Mexican government seeks it.

Finally, U.S. immigration policy affects Mexico more than any other country. Ten percent of Mexicans now live in the United States, and more than six million Mexican workers lack documentation. *Given the size of its migrant population, its proximity, and the importance of this issue for security as well as U.S.-Mexico relations, the Task Force urges the implementation of new guest worker programs, regularization of the status of illegal immigrants residing in the United States, and encouragement of legal circular migration, especially for agricultural workers.*

Address Venezuela through Multilateral Institutions

The anti-U.S. policies of President Chávez of Venezuela should be taken seriously by U.S. policymakers. It is important that the United States keep a close watch on Venezuela and that Chávez's potentially destabilizing policies within Latin America be carefully monitored. At the same time, a good deal of Venezuela's international support is limited to the concrete benefits that Venezuela provides, such as financial support, subsidized oil, and infrastructure investment. Thus, according to the most recent Latinobarómetro poll of Latin Americans, President Chávez's leadership ranks at the bottom, only slightly above lowest-ranked Fidel Castro. The 2007 Pew Global Attitudes Project indicates that nearly three-quarters of Brazilians, Peruvians, and Chileans doubt Chávez is doing "the right thing" in world affairs. This suggests the United States must temper its vigilance with a careful assessment of Chávez's real influence in the region.

U.S. policy is limited in its ability to sway either the domestic or foreign policy of Venezuela. Nevertheless, there are actions the United States can take to protect its interests in Latin America further. These include:

- Maintaining official relations with the Venezuelan government, both formal and informal, in order to keep channels open.

- Working through multilateral institutions, in particular the United Nations and the Organization of American States, to monitor democratic institutions and criticize antidemocratic behavior in Venezuela (and other countries).

- Increasing funding for "social justice" programs and policies in Latin America. Providing a U.S.-backed alternative to Chávez's vision will improve U.S. standing in the region and promote U.S. interests.

- Creating incentives for U.S. private sector investment in energy infrastructure in the region and U.S. leadership in the development of alternative fuels. This could both improve diplomatic relations with other countries in the region and help diversify U.S. energy consumption.

- Resist the temptation to react unilaterally to the results of Interpol's investigations in Colombia. Measures initiated by multilateral organizations, such as the United Nations, the European Union, and the

OAS, as well as diplomatic efforts by a number of countries in the Western Hemisphere, will be the most effective avenue against any country found to be supporting criminal and insurgent groups actively.

An emerging issue for U.S.–Venezuela relations centers on Hugo Chávez's recent announcement that Venezuela will pursue nuclear power. Given the increasingly authoritarian nature of the Venezuelan government and its close ties with Iran, this announcement is particularly troubling. In response to Venezuela, the United States should:

- Aggressively pursue already existing efforts such as collaborating with partners at the International Atomic Energy Agency and the Nuclear Suppliers Group to develop universal rules that constrain the spread of enrichment and reprocessing. This will be more effective than narrowly focusing on Venezuela, as the latter approach is unlikely to attract the multilateral support necessary for success.

- Focus on the most sensitive parts of Venezuela's potential nuclear program—uranium enrichment and plutonium reprocessing—with the aim of ensuring that no Venezuelan nuclear program involves capabilities on either front.

Open Informal and Formal Channels with Cuba

Cuba is an authoritarian state guilty of serious human rights violations. Human rights organizations estimate that there are between one hundred and two hundred political prisoners in Cuba today. In early 2008, Raúl Castro was elected by the Cuban National Assembly and its Council of State to become the president of the Council of State and of the republic. Within the framework of socialism, a number of measures designed to enhance the quality of people's lives and personal freedoms have followed. More, in the realm of shrinking the size of the state and boosting productivity and the creation of wealth, may follow. Fidel Castro's formal resignation and the stable succession of his brother as head of state have challenged the effectiveness of a half-century of U.S. economic sanctions, whether designed to destabilize or overthrow the regime, interrupt its continuity, or bring liberal democracy to the island.

The United States can play a positive role in promoting the values of an open society with policies that support the greater enjoyment of human rights by Cubans and lay the groundwork for a pluralistic future on the island. This could be facilitated by increasing contact between U.S. and Cuban citizens (including Cuban Americans and their families) through reducing current Department of Treasury travel restrictions. While increased trade might funnel more resources to the Cuban government and strengthen its short-term staying power, economic isolation has long provided Cuba's authorities with a convenient excuse for many of the island's core problems. The time is ripe to show the Cuban people, especially the younger generations, that an alternative exists to permanent hostility between these two nations and that the United States can play a positive role in Cuba's future. Given this, the United States should initiate a series of steps, with the aim of lifting the embargo against Cuba. The United States should:

- Permit freer travel to and facilitate trade with Cuba. The White House should repeal the 2004 restrictions placed on Cuban-American family travel and remittances.

- Reinstate and liberalize the thirteen categories of licensed people-to-people "purposeful travel" for other Americans, instituted by the Clinton administration in preparation for the 1998 papal visit to Havana.

- Hold talks on issues of mutual concern to both parties, such as migration, human smuggling, drug trafficking, public health, the future of the Guantánamo naval base, and on environmentally sustainable resource management, especially as Cuba, with a number of foreign oil companies, begins deep-water exploration for potentially significant reserves.

- Work more effectively with partners in the Western Hemisphere and in Europe to press Cuba on its human rights record and for more democratic reform.

- Mindful of the last one hundred years of U.S.-Cuba relations, assure Cubans on the island that the United States will pursue a respectful arm's-length relationship with a democratic Cuba.

- Repeal the 1996 Helms–Burton law, which removed most of the executive branch's authority to eliminate economic sanctions. While moving to repeal the law, the U.S. Congress should pass legislative measures, as it has with agricultural sales, designed to liberalize trade with and travel to Cuba, while supporting opportunities to strengthen democratic institutions there.

In pursuing the full range of U.S. objectives through the concrete policy recommendations laid out in this report, the United States must focus its efforts and resources on helping Latin America strengthen the public institutions necessary to address the identified challenges. In doing so, Washington should work in partnership with Latin American nations through multilateral organizations such as the World Bank, the Inter-American Development Bank, the International Monetary Fund, the International Finance Corporation, and the Organization of American States. It should also continue to work closely with civil society organizations and domestic and international businesses to create more inclusive economic, social, and political opportunities for Latin American countries and their citizens.

Achieving the ambitious goals of strengthening institutions and improving the lives of Latin Americans will require long-term efforts on the part of many participants, most importantly Latin American governments and societies themselves. Nevertheless, there is a significant supporting role for the United States. Expanding its policy framework and concentrating on strategic regional partnerships will best promote U.S. interests, enhancing stability, security, and prosperity throughout the hemisphere.

Additional View

I am pleased to endorse most of the analysis and recommendations of this report, and particularly welcome the proposals for U.S. immigration reform and for changes in U.S. policy toward Cuba. I thought, however, it would be helpful to offer these supplemental comments.

First, I believe that an effective redirection of U.S. policy in the hemisphere must be accompanied by a reshaping of Washington's global policies. Constructive relations with Latin American nations require that the United States respect international rules and multilateral arrangements, decrease reliance on military force, and end the use of torture (especially while preaching about human rights).

Second, the report, in my view, understates the economic and political gains that most Latin American nations have made in recent years, and overestimates the potential contributions of U.S. policy to further progress in many areas.

Third, I think that the report, while focusing on a set of critical challenges for Latin America, gives insufficient attention to, first, the importance of sustained and significant economic growth in the region to addressing all of these challenges, and, second, how the United States can help foster the needed growth by further opening its economy and working toward greater regional economic integration on trade, investment, and infrastructure. The targeted initiatives recommended in the report will be useful, but the United States can contribute most to Latin America and U.S.-Latin America relations by helping to create and sustain a broader environment for economic advance.

Peter Hakim

Task Force Members

Charlene Barshefsky is senior international partner at Wilmer Cutler Pickering Hale and Dorr LLP (WilmerHale) in Washington, DC. She joined the firm after serving as U.S. trade representative (USTR) from 1997 to 2001 and as acting and deputy USTR from 1993 to 1996. She serves on the boards of directors of American Express Company, the Estée Lauder Companies Inc., Intel Corporation, and Starwood Hotels & Resorts Worldwide, Inc. She also serves on the Board of the Council on Foreign Relations.

R. Rand Beers is currently president of the National Security Network and an adjunct lecturer on terrorism at the Kennedy School of Government at Harvard University. He most recently worked as the national security adviser for the Kerry-Edwards campaign. He served in four positions on the National Security Council (NSC) staff at the White House during four administrations. His functions included director for counterterrorism and counternarcotics, director for peacekeeping, and senior director for intelligence programs (1988–98), as well as assistant secretary of state for international narcotics and law enforcement affairs (1998–2002) and special assistant to the president and senior director for combating terrorism on the NSC staff (2002–2003).

Note: Task Force members participate in their individual and not their institutional capacities.
*The individual has endorsed the report and submitted an additional view.

Alberto R. Coll is professor of international law and director of the European legal studies program at the DePaul College of Law in Chicago. Before joining DePaul in 2005, he was chairman of the Strategic Research Department at the U.S. Naval War College in Newport, Rhode Island, where he also served for five years as dean of the Center for Naval Warfare Studies. From 1990 to 1993, Dr. Coll served as principal deputy assistant secretary of defense, overseeing the Defense Department's policy, strategy, and budget in the areas of special operations forces and "low-intensity" conflict, including counterterrorism. For his work, he received the Secretary of Defense Medal for Outstanding Public Service.

Margaret E. Crahan is Kozmetsky distinguished professor and director of the Kozmetsky Center of Excellence in Global Finance at St. Edward's University. From 1994 to 2008 she was the Dorothy Epstein professor at Hunter College and the Graduate Center of the City University of New York and from 1982 to 1994 she was the Henry R. Luce professor of religion, power and political process at Occidental College. She currently is vice president of the board of the Inter-American Institute of Human Rights. Dr. Crahan has done research on topics spanning the sixteenth through twentieth centuries and has published over one hundred articles and books.

Jose W. Fernandez is a partner and co-chairs the Latin America practice at Latham & Watkins LLP. For nearly three decades, his work has focused on Latin America, working on a wide variety of matters as the economies of the region have evolved. He has advised clients on financings, acquisitions, privatizations, securities offerings, and joint ventures across a number of Latin American countries. Mr. Fernandez serves on the board of directors of Dartmouth College, ACCION International, and the Council of the Americas, among others. He has been both chair of the ABA's Inter-American Law Committee and chair of the Committee on Inter-American Affairs of the New York City Bar. He is currently co-chair of the Cross Border M&A and Joint Ventures Committee of the New York State Bar Association, and a member of the Latin America Advisory Council of the ABA.

Francis Fukuyama is the Bernard L. Schwartz professor of international political economy at the Paul H. Nitze School of Advanced International Studies (SAIS) at the Johns Hopkins University and the director of SAIS's international development program. He is also chairman of the editorial board of a new magazine, the *American Interest*. Dr. Fukuyama was a member of the president's Council on Bioethics from 2001 to 2005. He is a member of advisory boards for the National Endowment for Democracy, the *Journal of Democracy,* and the New America Foundation.

Peter Hakim* is president of the Inter-American Dialogue, the leading U.S. center for policy analysis and exchange on Western Hemisphere affairs. He was a vice president of the Inter-American Foundation and worked for the Ford Foundation in both New York and Latin America. Mr. Hakim has taught at MIT and Columbia. He currently serves on boards and advisory committees for the Foundation of the Americas, the World Bank, the Inter-American Development Bank, *Foreign Affairs en Español*, Intellibridge Corporation, and Human Rights Watch.

James A. Harmon is chairman of Harmon & Co., a financial advisory firm organized in 2001, and chairman of the Caravel Fund (International) Ltd., an emerging markets fund. Mr. Harmon served as chairman, president, and CEO of the Export-Import Bank of the United States from 1997 to 2001. Prior to entering government services Mr. Harmon was chairman and CEO of the investment bank Wertheim Schroder. In 2004, Mr. Harmon was elected chairman of the World Resources Institute. Mr. Harmon is a senior adviser to the Rothschild Group and is a member of its European Advisory Council. Mr. Harmon is a member of the board of directors of Questar Corporation and the Alfa Bank (Moscow) Capital Partners Board. Mr. Harmon is also a member of the boards of the School of International and Public Affairs (SIPA) at Columbia University, Africare, and the Center for Global Development, and a trustee emeritus of Brown University and Barnard College.

John G. Heimann is the founding chairman of the Financial Stability Institute of the Bank for International Settlements and now serves as its senior adviser. He was a founding partner of Warburg Pincus & Co., and later the chairman of the Financial Institutions Group and member of the executive committee of Merrill Lynch & Co. Mr. Heimann has served as U.S. comptroller of the currency, superintendent of banks for New York State, and chairman of the Federal Deposit Insurance Corporation. He is a member of the Group of Thirty.

James T. Hill retired as a four-star general in the U.S. Army after having served since 1968. From 2002 to 2004 he was the combatant commander of the U.S. Southern Command, commanding all U.S. military operations and relationships in the Caribbean and Central and South America. In assignment related to Latin America, General Hill also served as deputy commanding general of the Multinational Force in Haiti (1994–95) and assistant deputy director for politico-military affairs on the Joint Staff (1992–94). Currently he is the president of the JT Hill Group, a strategic consulting firm located in Miami, Florida.

Donna Hrinak is the director for corporate and government affairs in Latin America for Kraft Foods Inc. She joined Kraft in 2006 after working with the international advisory firm McLarty Associates, where she was senior director. She also worked as the co-chair of the International Trade and Competition practice group at the law firm of Steel Hector & Davis. From 1974 to 2004, Ambassador Hrinak served as a U.S. Foreign Service officer. She completed her Foreign Service career as ambassador to Brazil and also served as ambassador to Venezuela, Bolivia, and the Dominican Republic and as deputy assistant secretary of state for Mexico and the Caribbean. In 1994, she served as coordinator for policy for the Miami Summit of the Americas. In addition to her Foreign Service assignments, Hrinak has worked in the office of Representative Patricia Schroeder on a fellowship from the American Political Science Association. Hrinak serves on the boards of the Inter-American Dialogue and the Pan American Development Foundation and on the board of counselors of McLarty Associates.

James V. Kimsey created America Online, Inc., and currently serves as chairman emeritus. In 1996, he launched the Kimsey Foundation, which provides grants that benefit the Washington, DC, community in areas from arts to education. Mr. Kimsey received presidential appointments to the Kennedy Center board of trustees and the West Point board of visitors. In 2001, Secretary of State Colin Powell named Mr. Kimsey as chairman of the International Commission on Missing Persons. Mr. Kimsey also serves as chairman emeritus of Refugees International and as a member of the board of the International Crisis Group.

Jim Kolbe served in the U.S. House of Representatives from 1985 to 2007, representing the Tucson area. A Republican, Mr. Kolbe served for twenty years on the House Appropriations Committee. He was also chairman of the Treasury, Post Office, and Related Agencies subcommittee for four years, and for the last six years in Congress, he chaired the Foreign Operations, Export Financing, and Related Agencies subcommittee. Congressman Kolbe is currently a senior adviser at McLarty Associates and serves as a senior transatlantic fellow for the German Marshall Fund of the United States and as an adjunct professor in the College of Business at the University of Arizona.

Kellie Meiman leads the Brazil/Southern Cone practice of the international advisory firm McLarty Associates. She worked most recently at the Office of the U.S. Trade Representative (USTR) as director for Mercosur and the Southern Cone, where she had primary responsibility for Brazil, Argentina, Chile, Paraguay, and Uruguay. Prior to her work at USTR, Ms. Meiman served as a Foreign Service officer with the U.S. Department of State.

Shannon K. O'Neil is the fellow for Latin America studies at the Council on Foreign Relations. Before joining the Council, she was a justice, welfare, and economics fellow and an executive committee member and graduate associate at the Weatherhead Center for International Affairs at Harvard University. She was also a Fulbright Scholar in Mexico and Argentina. Prior to her academic work, Dr. O'Neil worked in the private sector as an equity analyst at Indosuez Capital Latin America and Credit Lyonnais Securities.

María Otero is president and CEO of ACCION International. Ms. Otero chairs the board of ACCION Investments, co-chairs the Microenterprise Coalition, and serves on the boards of directors of three regulated microfinance institutions in Latin America. She chaired the board of Bread for the World from 1992 to 1997. In 1994, President Clinton appointed Ms. Otero to serve as chair of the board of directors of the Inter-American Foundation, a position she held until January 2000. She has also served in an advisory capacity to the World Bank's Consultative Group to Assist the Poorest.

Arturo C. Porzecanski is a professor of international finance and distinguished economist-in-residence at American University's School of International Service, having previously taught at Columbia University, New York University, and Williams College. He is a member of the board of directors of the Tinker Foundation and of the Washington Office on Latin America. Prior to his current academic career, Dr. Porzecanski worked for nearly three decades as an international economist on Wall Street, starting out with J.P. Morgan in the 1970s, where he served as economic adviser on Latin America. He later rose to become chief economist for emerging markets at several financial institutions, the last of which was the European banking group ABN AMRO.

David J. Rothkopf is president and chief executive officer of Garten Rothkopf, a Washington, DC–based international advisory firm serving the investment, corporate, and government communities. He is also a visiting scholar at the Carnegie Endowment for International Peace, where he is chairman of the Carnegie Economic Strategy Roundtable. He is author of *Running the World: The Inside Story of the National Security Council and the Architects of American Power; The Superclass: The Global Power Elite and the World They are Making;* and the forthcoming *Power, Inc.: The Untold Story of the Global Power Struggle Between Companies, Countries and Their Leaders.* He served as deputy undersecretary of commerce for international trade policy development and later as acting undersecretary of commerce for international trade during the Clinton administration. Rothkopf is a member of the advisory boards of the United States Institute of Peace, the Center for Global Development, and the Johns Hopkins/Bloomberg School of Public Health, and he is an adjunct professor of international affairs at Columbia University.

Julia E. Sweig served as senior adviser for this Task Force report. She is the Nelson and David Rockefeller senior fellow for Latin America studies and director of Latin America studies at the Council on Foreign Relations. Dr. Sweig is the author of *Friendly Fire: Losing Friends and Making Enemies in the Anti-American Century* and *Inside the Cuban Revolution,* as well as numerous scholarly articles, opinion pieces, congressional testimony, and CFR reports on Cuba, Venezuela, the Andes, Latin America, and American foreign policy. She serves on the editorial board of *Foreign Affairs en Español* and as a consultant on Latin American affairs for the Aspen Institute.

Task Force Observers

Laurie A. Garrett
Council on Foreign Relations

Eric Jacobstein
House Subcommittee on Western Hemisphere

Jamal A. Khokhar
Inter-American Development Bank

Daniel Kurtz-Phelan
Foreign Affairs

J. Patrick Maher
National Intelligence Council

Carl E. Meacham
Senate Committee on Foreign Relations

Janice O'Connell
Stonebridge International LLC

Jennifer J. Simon Butler
Senate Committee on Foreign Relations

Jason Steinbaum
House Subcommittee on Western Hemisphere

David G. Victor
Council on Foreign Relations

Mark Walker
Office of Representative Daniel Burton

Recent Independent Task Force Reports
Sponsored by the Council on Foreign Relations

U.S.-China Relations: An Affirmative Agenda, A Responsible Course (2007); Carla A. Hills and Dennis C. Blair, Chairs; Frank Sampson Jannuzi, Project Director

National Security Consequences of U.S. Oil Dependency (2006); John Deutch and James R. Schlesinger, Chairs; David G. Victor, Project Director

Russia's Wrong Direction: What the United States Can and Should Do (2006); John Edwards and Jack Kemp, Chairs; Stephen Sestanovich, Project Director

More than Humanitarianism: A Strategic U.S. Approach Toward Africa (2006); Anthony Lake and Christine Todd Whitman, Chairs; Princeton N. Lyman and J. Stephen Morrison, Project Directors

In the Wake of War: Improving U.S. Post-Conflict Capabilities (2005); Samuel R. Berger and Brent Scowcroft, Chairs; William L. Nash, Project Director; Mona K. Sutphen, Deputy Director

In Support of Arab Democracy: Why and How (2005); Madeleine K. Albright and Vin Weber, Chairs; Steven A. Cook, Project Director

Building a North American Community (2005); John P. Manley, Pedro Aspe, and William F. Weld, Chairs; Thomas P. d'Aquino, Andrés Rozental, and Robert A. Pastor, Vice Chairs; Chappel A. Lawson, Project Director; Cosponsored with the Canadian Council of Chief Executives and the Consejo Mexicano de Asuntos Internationales

Iran: Time for a New Approach (2004); Zbigniew Brzezinski and Robert M. Gates, Chairs; Suzanne Maloney, Project Director

Renewing the Atlantic Partnership (2004); Henry A. Kissinger and Lawrence H. Summers, Chairs; Charles A. Kupchan, Project Director

Nonlethal Weapons and Capabilities (2004); Graham T. Allison and Paul X. Kelley, Chairs; Richard L. Garwin, Project Director

New Priorities in South Asia: U.S. Policy Toward India, Pakistan, and Afghanistan (2003); Frank G.Wisner II, Nicholas Platt, and Marshall M. Bouton, Chairs; Dennis Kux and Mahnaz Ispahani, Project Directors; Cosponsored with the Asia Society

Finding America's Voice: A Strategy for Reinvigorating U.S. Public Diplomacy (2003); Peter G. Peterson, Chair; Jennifer Sieg, Project Director

Emergency Responders: Drastically Underfunded, Dangerously Unprepared (2003); Warren B. Rudman, Chair; Richard A. Clarke, Senior Adviser; Jamie F. Metzl, Project Director

Chinese Military Power (2003); Harold Brown, Chair; Joseph W. Prueher, Vice Chair; Adam Segal, Project Director

Iraq: The Day After (2003); Thomas R. Pickering and James R. Schlesinger, Chairs; Eric P. Schwartz, Project Director

Threats to Democracy (2002); Madeleine K. Albright and Bronislaw Geremek, Chairs; Morton H. Halperin, Project Director; Elizabeth Frawley Bagley, Associate Director

America—Still Unprepared, Still in Danger (2002); Gary Hart and Warren B. Rudman, Chairs; Stephen Flynn, Project Director

Terrorist Financing (2002); Maurice R. Greenberg, Chair; William F.Wechsler and Lee S.Wolosky, Project Directors

Enhancing U.S. Leadership at the United Nations (2002); David Dreier and Lee H. Hamilton, Chairs; Lee Feinstein and Adrian Karatnycky, Project Directors

Testing North Korea: The Next Stage in U.S. and ROK Policy (2001); Morton I. Abramowitz and James T. Laney, Chairs; Robert A. Manning, Project Director

The United States and Southeast Asia: A Policy for the New Administration (2001); J. Robert Kerrey, Chair; Robert A. Manning, Project Director

Strategic Energy Policy: Challenges for the 21ˢᵗ Century (2001); Edward L. Morse, Chair; Amy Myers Jaffe, Project Director

---

All publications listed are available on the Council on Foreign Relations website, CFR.org.
To order printed copies, contact the Brookings Institution Press: 800-537-5487.